THE COMPLETE PRACTICAL GUIDE TO
DIGITAL PHOTOGRAPHY

THE COMPLETE PRACTICAL GUIDE TO
DIGITAL PHOTOGRAPHY
STEP-BY-STEP TECHNIQUES AND TIPS

HOW TO TAKE PROFESSIONAL-QUALITY IMAGES WITH YOUR DIGITAL CAMERA,
INCLUDING EXPERT ADVICE AND OVER 500 CLEAR PHOTOGRAPHS

STEVE LUCK

southwater

This edition is published by Southwater, an imprint of
Anness Publishing Ltd, Blaby Road, Wigston,
Leicestershire LE18 4SE
Email: info@anness.com

Web: www.southwaterbooks.com; www.annesspublishing.com

Anness Publishing has a new picture agency outlet for images
for publishing, promotions or advertising. Please visit our
website www.practicalpictures.com for more information.

Publisher: Joanna Lorenz
Project Editor: Elizabeth Young
Proofreading Manager: Lindsay Zamponi
Production Controller: Christine Ni

Designed and produced for Anness Publishing by
The Bridgewater Book Company Limited
Art Director: Lisa McCormick
Project Editor: Polita Caaveiro
Designer: Kevin Knight

Ethical Trading Policy
At Anness Publishing we believe that business should be conducted
in an ethical and ecologically sustainable way, with respect for the
environment and a proper regard to the replacement of the natural
resources we employ.

As a publisher, we use a lot of wood pulp to make high-quality paper
for printing, and that wood commonly comes from spruce trees. We are
therefore currently growing more than 750,000 trees in three Scottish
forest plantations: Berrymoss (130 hectares/320 acres), West Touxhill
(125 hectares/305 acres) and Deveron Forest (75 hectares/185 acres).
The forests we manage contain more than 3.5 times the number of trees
employed each year in making paper for the books we manufacture.

Because of this ongoing ecological investment programme, you, as our
customer, can have the pleasure and reassurance of knowing that a tree
is being cultivated on your behalf to naturally replace the materials used
to make the book you are holding.

Our forestry programme is run in accordance with the UK Woodland
Assurance Scheme (UKWAS) and will be certified by the internationally
recognized Forest Stewardship Council (FSC). The FSC is a
non-government organization dedicated to promoting responsible
management of the world's forests. Certification ensures forests are
managed in an environmentally sustainable and socially responsible
way. For further information about this scheme, go to
www.annesspublishing.com/trees

© Anness Publishing Ltd 2011

Previously published as part of a larger volume, *The Complete
Illustrated Encyclopedia of Digital Photography*

Publisher's Note
Although the advice and information in this book are believed to be
accurate and true at the time of going to press, neither the authors nor
the publisher can accept any legal responsibility or liability for any errors
or omissions that may have been made nor for any inaccuracies nor for
any loss, harm or injury that comes about from following instructions or
advice in this book.

Introduction

Digital cameras and photography have come a long way in a short amount of time. Today, anyone thinking of buying an 'all-purpose' camera is more likely to consider buying a digital camera rather than a film camera, as digital cameras can do things that film cameras cannot – they can record sounds, videos and images, and they can display an image on the screen immediately after taking.

A digital world

To keep sales of their cameras ticking over, camera manufacturers – many of whom are running scared at the inexorable rise of the camera-phone – are developing cameras that make it increasingly easy for us to take well-exposed, sharply focused images. Sophisticated metering and auto-focusing systems, together with face

▼ Learning to take great photographs involves seeing in a different way. We are surrounded by a world of picture possibilities, but some are far better than others.

detection and anti-shake technologies, mean that technically incompetent shots are becoming a thing of the past. But we need to be wary of an over-reliance on such technology if we're to improve as photographers and to really enjoy what can be a satisfying and rewarding pastime.

Being able to take as many photographs as we like, pretty much with financial impunity, can be seen as a double-edged sword. On the one hand, it encourages experimentation – and you only have to look at a website such as Flickr (www.flickr.com) to see some of the hugely creative things people achieve with their digital cameras, which are unlikely to have come about without the digital revolution. On the other hand, it also encourages an almost 'scatter-gun' approach to photography – keep firing and sooner or later you're bound to come up with some interesting images. Although there's nothing inherently wrong with such an approach, it does in many ways negate the need or desire to learn. We need to slow down and look at our images in a more considered way – why does one shot 'work' when another from the same sequence fails? Why doesn't the image appear so full of movement? Why are the vibrant colours less intense? If we do this, we're going to increase our success rate, and by analysing what exactly it is about certain images that makes them stand out from the rest, we can mix the visual components a little to see what else works, and in that way our experimentation has some reason and method to it.

Close up or Macro is a feature of digital cameras. This allows you to take close-up pictures of very small objects such as flowers, small animals and insects.

▶ Colourful subjects can lend themselves well to black and white photography. Digital cameras feature a Black and White mode, which allows you to shoot black and white.

Capture the scene

In this book the technical has been deliberately mixed with the creative. To be a good digital photographer it helps to have a thorough understanding of your equipment, particularly if you're either new to digital cameras or have 'upgraded' from a simple point-and-shoot to a more complex model. To the uninitiated, the often mind-boggling settings and options might seem surplus to requirements, but most are there for a very good reason and it pays to spend some time learning how they work and what they do. But this technical knowledge would come to nothing without having some idea about what to point the lens at. If you're reading this, then it's safe to assume that you have an appreciation for images and sights that you've seen and a desire to capture them in a way that most accurately reflects both how they appeared to you and what they meant to you.

The intention of this book is to provide you with a good technical knowledge of what your equipment is capable of producing. It explains how best to creatively translate the scene in front of you into a distilled, two-dimensional replica that elicits the sense of time and place. Interspersed along the way are exercises that help you to put the theory into practice.

 Children make fascinating subjects, but it can be difficult to get a good picture, so you will need to persevere and take lots of shots.

▶ When on holiday ensure that you have a lightweight and well-protected kit to hand as you never know when the opportunity for a great shot will come up.

The Digital Environment

The 'language' of digital photography can sometimes seem at best baffling and, at worst, impenetrable. Is it really necessary to know all the technical jargon? While not essential, a grasp of the language of digital imaging will help you to navigate around the digital environment more smoothly, and to understand the technical requirements for a good-looking image. In this chapter, we'll look at the physical make-up of a digital image, and how it is captured and stored, and finish with a rundown of the most popular digital cameras and various lenses available to today's photographers.

Pixels and Resolution

All digital images are composed of minute blocks known as 'pixels', which is short for 'picture elements'. An individual pixel carries information that governs its colour, the strength of that colour, and how light the pixel is displayed or printed – three aspects that are usually referred to as the pixel's Hue, Saturation and Brightness (HSB) values. Because most digital images are made up of millions of pixels they are not usually visible to the naked eye, so when we look at a digital image we see the gradual and subtle changes in light and shade, and tone and colour as smooth transitions, or 'continuous tones'.

The number of pixels that an image has dictates the image's resolution (how much detail it contains) and the more pixels, the higher the resolution. The number of pixels also relates to the maximum print size, as more pixels mean you can achieve a larger print size. It is for this reason that resolution is one of the key factors governing the quality of digital images, but as we shall see later, the number of pixels in the image is by no means the only factor.

Print resolution

The resolution of a digital image is measured in pixels per inch (ppi), and the standard resolution to achieve photo-quality prints is 300ppi. So, if you know how many megapixels (millions of pixels) a digital camera has, it's simple to work out the optimum print size the camera is capable of producing. For example, let's assume a 6 megapixel (6MP) camera has a sensor with 2,816 pixels across by 2,112 pixels down (6 million pixels in total). To work out the optimum print size the camera is capable of, simply divide 2,816 and 2,112 pixels by 300ppi. This gives you $9^1/_2$ and 7. Therefore, a 6MP camera is capable of producing a print measuring $9^1/_2$ x 7in (24 x 18cm).

It's important to remember, however, that 300ppi is considered to be the optimum industry-standard resolution. Depending on the image, the camera, the printer and the intended size of the print (larger prints tend to be viewed from farther away), you may find that a resolution of 200ppi (or lower) can produce perfectly acceptable results.

Screen resolution

Because a computer's monitor has a standard resolution of either 72ppi (Windows) or 96ppi (Macintosh), images from a digital camera that are to be viewed on screen can be set to the same 72ppi or 96ppi resolution (which are extremely low in terms of print) and will still appear as continuous-tone images when viewed on screen.

In terms of image size, it follows that with a monitor resolution that is set to 800 x 600 pixels, the image from the camera only needs to be 800 x 600 pixels for the image to fill the screen completely.

Digital colour

Almost all the colours in a digital image are made by combining the three additive primary colours – red, green and blue – often referred to as the RGB colour model. For the vast majority of digital images, each of these three colours has 256 different shades ranging from 0 to 255.

Digitally, each of these colours is known as a channel, and a typical digital image that can display up to 16.7 million colours is often described

▶ **RIGHT** The more pixels that are used to make up an image, the more detail is visible and the smoother the image appears. In this sequence of images, the number of pixels in the image has been halved each time, but the image's physical size has remained the same. As the number of pixels decreases so detail is lost and the pixels become increasingly visible – so that by the final image, it's possible to see the individual pixels that make up the image.

320 x 320 pixels

160 x 160 pixels

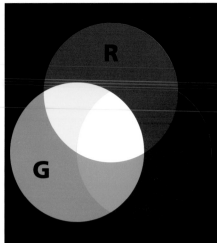

as having 8 bits per channel or 24-bit colour (the total of each of the three channels having 8 bits of colour). The term 'bit' stands for 'binary digit', the basic unit of computing.

Bits utilize the binary counting system in which '0' equals 'off' and '1' represents 'on'. A true 1-bit image would only be made of either '0' (off or black) or '1' (on or white), while a 2-bit image would be made up of '00' (black), '11' (white) and '01' (grey) or '10' (a different grey). By the time we get up to 8 bits, there are 254 additional greys in between black and white. Substitute the white, black and greys for one of the red, green and blue channels and you have a combination of different colours made up of 256 (red) multiplied by 256 (green) multiplied by 256 (blue), or 16.7 million colours in total.

ABOVE This screen shot taken from an image-editing program shows the image used in the sequence below broken into its three red, green and blue channels. All colour digital images use the 'RGB colour model' to show more or less all the colours the human eye can see.

ABOVE The additive primary colours – red, green and blue – are the colours of natural light, and can be used to make up just about all the colours our eyes are able to differentiate. This is why the RGB model is used in digital imaging to represent most of the colours of the visible spectrum.

MEGAPIXELS VERSUS PRINT SIZE

Camera	Pixels	Approximate print size at 300ppi	Approximate print size at 200ppi
3MP	2,048 x 1,536	7 x 5in (18 x 13cm)	10 x 7½in (26 x 19cm)
4MP	2,280 x 1,700	7½ x 5½in (19 x 14cm)	11½ x 8½in (29 x 22cm)
5MP	2,592 x 1,944	8½ x 6½in (22 x 16cm)	13 x 9½in (33 x 24cm)
6MP	2,816 x 2,112	9½ x 7in (24 x 18cm)	14 x 10½in (36 x 27cm)
7MP	3,072 x 2,304	10 x 7½in (25 x 19cm)	15½ x 11½in (39 x 29cm)
8MP	3,264 x 2,448	11 x 8in (28 x 20cm)	16½ x 12in (42x 30cm)
10MP	3,888 x 2,592	13 x 8½in (33 x 22cm)	19½ x 13in (49 x 33cm)
12MP	4,288 x 2,848	14½ x 9½in (37 x 24cm)	21½ x 14in (55 x 36cm)

80 x 80 pixels

40 x 40 pixels

20 x 20 pixels

Camera Sensors

A digital camera's sensor takes on the same function as film does in a conventional camera. The sensor is where the camera's lens focuses the subject or scene and it is where the image is initially 'captured' before being converted to digital data and relayed to the camera's memory card for longer-term storage.

Anatomy of the sensor

The surface of the sensor is covered with a grid of millions of microscopic, light-recording devices called 'photosites'. Each photosite represents one pixel of the captured image. When manufacturers refer to an 8MP camera, the camera's sensor has approximately 8 million photosites.

One of the key components of a photosite is the photodiode, which converts light into an electrical charge – the stronger the light, the greater the charge. The array of photosites records the various light levels and converts them to corresponding, electrical charges. These electrical charges are then amplified and sent to an analogue to digital (A/D) converter, where the charge is converted into digital data.

Seeing red, green and blue

Photosites record light intensity, but cannot differentiate between light of different wavelengths, and cannot, therefore, record colour. To generate a colour image, a thin filter is placed over the layer of photodiodes. Known as a colour filter array (CFA), the filter is a mosaic of red, green and blue squares, with each square sitting directly above a photodiode. With a CFA in place, each photosite is able to record varying intensities of red, green or blue light. To make up an almost full spectrum of colours, the camera's processor analyses the colour and intensity of each photosite, then compares it with the colour and intensity of its direct neighbours. In this way, the processor interpolates, or 'estimates', a much more accurate colour for each pixel. This complex and sophisticated interpolation

▲ **ABOVE** A CCD sensor from a digital SLR. The image area measures 1 x ⅔in (2.54 x 1.67cm) but contains 6.3 million individual photosites, or pixels.

process is known as 'demosaicing' and is how each pixel in the image can display one of 16.7 million colours.

Processing and formatting

Once the demosaicing interpolation process is complete, the image undergoes further processing, which may, for example, enhance colours, adjust brightness and contrast, or even sharpen the image depending on the camera's settings. Once these adjustments have been applied, the data is then formatted and fed to the camera's memory card for storage.

▼ **BELOW** Millions of photodiodes cover a digital sensor. A coloured filter enables it to record colour, while the microlens optimizes the light from the camera lens.

A single photosite

Three colour-filtered photosites

SENSOR TYPES

Almost all digital cameras use one of two types of sensor – a complementary metal oxide semiconductor (CMOS), or a charge-coupled device (CCD). Both sensors are made in a similar way and both capture an image as described on these pages. The principal difference between the two is how the information from each photosite is processed.

In a CCD, each row of photosites is connected or 'coupled'. After an image is taken, the accumulated charge value from each photosite is passed down row-by-row and read at one corner of the array before being deleted. The values are then fed to another chip for the analogue to digital (A/D) conversion to take place.

In a CMOS chip, each photosite is equipped with its own amplifiers and circuitry so that the charge value can be read directly from each individual photosite before passing directly to the A/D converter. Each type of sensor has its own benefits and drawbacks. Historically, CCDs, which are the more common of the two types, were more efficient at gathering light and tended to produce higher-quality images, while CMOS sensors were cheaper to manufacture and were more energy efficient.

In recent years, manufacturers of both systems have worked hard to improve their systems and it is now very difficult to say that one works significantly better than the other.

A 'coupled' CCD sensor array

last row read

first row read

A CMOS has individual amplifiers

THE COLOUR FILTER ARRAY (CFA)

As an image sensor's photodiodes can only recognize shades of grey, a colour filter array (CFA) is placed over the sensor so the photodiodes record red, green or blue light. There are twice as many green squares as either of the other colours, because the human eye is much more sensitive to green light. The most commonly used pattern in today's CFAs is called the Bayer pattern, after the Kodak technician who invented it.

incoming light

sensor layer

Bayer pattern

Filters enable a photodiode to 'see' colour

Bayer pattern filter array

SENSOR SIZE

It's important to know that sensor sizes vary enormously from camera to camera and this can impact on the quality of digital images. For example, there are a number of digital cameras on the market featuring 12MP sensors, but this doesn't mean that the sensors are the same size. This is quite significant because the physical size of the sensor determines the size of its individual photosites. To fit 12 million photosites on a smaller sensor they have to be much smaller. Smaller photosites are less sensitive to light, less able to capture very dark or very light areas of a scene accurately, and can result in increased levels of 'noise' (see pages 14–15). The images show the relative size of the common sensors used in today's digital cameras. Some advanced dSLRs have 'full-frame' sensors, which are the same size as a frame of 35mm film.

Designated sensor type	Sensor's dimensions

1–2.5-in sensor = 5.8 x 4.3mm

1–1.8-in sensor = 7.2 x 5.3mm

2–3-in sensor = 8.8 x 6.6mm

Typical dSLR sensor = 23.5 x 15.7mm

Full-frame dSLR = 36 x 24mm

ISO, Sensitivity and Noise

Those who are familiar with film photography will know that different films have different ISO (or ASA) ratings. The ISO (International Standards Organization) rating determines how sensitive the film is to light – the higher the rating, the more sensitive the film. Similarly, the sensor in a digital camera can also be adjusted to be more or less sensitive to light, and helpfully this is given as an equivalent ISO rating or setting. A compact camera, for example, may have ISO settings of 50, 100, 200 and 400, while a digital SLR will often feature incremental settings of 100, 200, 400, 800, 1600 and 3200. As with ISO ratings for film, the higher the digital camera's ISO setting, the more sensitive the sensor is to light, but in reality this means the signal created by light striking the sensor is amplified to a greater degree.

dSLR at ISO 100

dSLR at ISO 200

dSLR at ISO 400

dSLR at ISO 800   dSLR at ISO 1600

dSLR at ISO 3200

ABOVE This shot of rooftops over Prague was taken in late afternoon, low-light conditions. A high ISO setting of 800 was used to ensure a shutter speed of $\frac{1}{60}$ sec could be used to avoid camera shake. The result, however, is a 'noisy' image, characterized by an unpleasant speckled effect that is more noticeable in the darker areas of the red roof tiles, clearly shown in the inset image.

LEFT This series of images shows how 'noise' increases with higher ISO settings. These images were taken from a dSLR. Those on the opposite page were shot with a high-specification compact camera. At a low ISO and small print size there's little difference between the two.

Low light

The benefit of being able to increase a camera's ISO setting is apparent in low-light situations, such as indoors or outdoors in dark or very overcast conditions. In such circumstances (and where using flash or a tripod is not an option), if the camera is set with a low ISO setting of 50 or 100, the camera would have to have a slow shutter speed of, for example, $^1/_8$ or $^1/_{15}$ of a second (sec), or an increased lens aperture size (see pages 76–77). At these slow shutter speeds you run the real risk of the camera moving slightly as you take the picture, which results in a blurry image. This usually undesirable effect is commonly referred to as 'camera shake'. Alternatively, your subject may move during the exposure, again resulting in a blurred image.

High ISO

There is a direct correlation between shutter speed and ISO setting. By increasing the ISO setting, the shutter speed increases proportionately, so that, for example, from $^1/_{15}$ sec at ISO 50, the shutter speed increases to $^1/_{30}$ sec at ISO 100, $^1/_{60}$ sec at ISO 200, $^1/_{125}$ sec at ISO 400 and $^1/_{250}$ sec at ISO 800. At these later speeds, you'll avoid camera shake and 'freeze' most human movement. You can adjust the ISO between shots to suit the shooting conditions.

Noise

Unfortunately, there is a drawback to using high ISO settings and comparisons can be drawn with conventional film photography. Photographers who use 'fast' film (film with a high ISO rating), will end up with speckled or 'grainy' prints. Likewise, in digital photography, increasing the ISO setting amplifies the electronic signal from the sensor, but will also amplify the background electronic 'noise' that is present in the camera's circuitry and result in interference – think of it as 'visible hissing'. This distorts the image signal and creates a speckled or 'noisy' image, which, unlike certain film 'graininess', is rarely pleasant to look at.

Low ISO

It's sensible to use the lowest ISO setting that will still allow a fast enough shutter speed to avoid camera shake and resulting blurred images. Alternatively, use a tripod, as you'll be able to use a lower ISO setting and slower shutter speed than is possible when holding the camera. If you're using slow shutter speeds use the camera's 'Noise Reduction' facility if it has one.

Noise and sensor size

Larger sensors, such as those found on digital SLRs (dSLRs), are less prone to 'noise'. This is because the larger photosites found on such sensors collect light more effectively and thus don't need as much amplification (high ISO) to capture a poorly lit scene as a small sensor. In addition, because photosites are set farther apart on larger sensors, increasing the ISO setting will cause less overall interference, and so create less noise. Therefore, you can obtain acceptable results from a dSLR when the ISO is set at 800 or 1600 – settings that are unavailable on many compacts.

Auto ISO

Most cameras will have an automatic ISO option. When selected, the camera will monitor the shutter speed and if the speed drops below the point at which camera shake may occur (usually around $^1/_{30}$ sec), it will automatically increase the ISO setting. This can help you avoid taking blurred images, but it can also introduce noise. On some cameras the automatic ISO range is limited, so the camera avoids using very high ISO settings. Remember, manually set the lowest possible ISO if you're using a tripod as there's no danger of camera shake and you'll get noise-free images.

▼ **BELOW** At higher ISO settings (or larger print sizes), the differences between a digital compact camera's small sensor and the larger sensor of a dSLR become much more obvious. The compact camera suffers from far more 'noise', resulting in coloured speckles appearing in images.

| Compact at ISO 100 | Compact at ISO 200 | Compact at ISO 800 | Compact at ISO 3200 |

File Formats

As the light from a captured image passes through a digital camera it is turned into digital information. For this to be safely stored and retrieved, it must be digitally organized, or formatted. For those new to digital photography, the file formats and associated quality and size settings available in a camera's menu can be bewildering – not helped by the use of technical-looking abbreviations such as .JPG or .TIF – but in reality they are quite straightforward.

JPEG

Pronounced 'jay-peg', the JPEG format (.JPG/.jpg being the file extension) is the most widely used image format due to its versatility. JPEG stands for Joint Photographic Experts Group after the committee that developed the format. JPEGs are able to 'compress' the image files and so reduce their size. This allows you to fit more images on to the memory card. Most digital cameras use the JPEG format and allow you to select the amount of compression applied to the image. This is often expressed as 'High/ Medium/Low' or 'Fine/Normal'. However described, it should be clear which setting will apply the most compression, as the more the image is compressed the greater the amount of picture information that is lost.

Sophisticated interpolation algorithms, known as 'lossy' compression, assess which pixel information can be discarded without overly degrading the image. The trade-off for having more images on a memory card is reduced image quality, but depending on how the images are going to be viewed, the level of detail lost may be negligible. You'll need to experiment with the settings to find the most appropriate level of compression suitable for your needs. If storage space is an issue, you'll want a high level of compression, but if image quality is the overriding factor, you should opt for a low level.

Resolution

Don't confuse the compression setting with the resolution setting (in other words the physical dimensions of the image). The menus for both are often combined into one setting 'Large/ Medium', or 'Small/Fine'. The first refers to the image size (in pixels) and the second refers to the amount of compression applied. More compression means smaller files, but lower quality.

▶ **RIGHT** Basic JPEG files produce the smallest files. Fine compression gives the best JPEG image. Normal files are a good compromise.

Basic JPEG compression

Fine JPEG compression

Normal JPEG compression

IMAGE-RECORDING QUALITY

This table shows image settings, resultant file and print sizes (at 240ppi) and the number of images that can be stored on a 500MB card for a typical 8MP camera.

Image-recording quality	File format	File size in pixels and MB	Print size	No. of shots
Large/Fine	JPEG	3,504 x 2,336 (3.6MB)	A3 or larger	132
Large/Normal	JPEG	3,504 x 2,336 (1.8MB)	A3 or larger	266
Medium/Fine	JPEG	2,544 x 1,696 (2.2MB)	A5 > A4	224
Medium/Normal	JPEG	2,544 x 1,696 (1.1MB)	A5 > A4	442
Small/Fine	JPEG	1,728 x 1,152 (1.2MB)	A5 or smaller	390
Small/Normal	JPEG	1,728 x 1,152 (0.6MB)	A5 or smaller	760
RAW	RAW	3,504 x 2,336 (8.7MB)	A3 or larger	54

RAW + JPEG

Some cameras, particularly the higher-end models, provide a RAW and JPEG setting, usually called 'RAW + JPEG'. When using this setting, the camera will produce two files for every image captured – a RAW file, which is the unprocessed data recorded by the camera's sensor, and which can be saved on to a computer for further editing, and also a JPEG image that can be sent directly to a printer.

▲ **ABOVE** Software for editing RAW images allows you to fine-tune your image's settings before saving for printing.

Processing

When images are saved as JPEGs, they will usually be adjusted by the camera's internal processors before being saved to the memory card. The specific processes and the level at which they're applied will depend on the camera and the settings you choose, but colours may be boosted, contrast and brightness levels adjusted, and the image may be sharpened. The idea behind these internal processes is that they help to ensure that any images stored on the memory card can be printed without further digital editing work on a computer. Most cameras will allow you to adjust the level of processing, but it's important to try out the various settings.

TIFF

The TIFF format (.TIF/.tif) is rarely available on digital cameras, but it's an important format as it is the industry standard. Most photographs that are published in books and magazines are saved as TIFF files, and almost all image-editing software allows you to save files as TIFFs. The reason TIFF is an important format is that no information is lost when the image is saved (unlike JPEGs). In other words, it is a 'lossless' file format. As a result, TIFFs are capable of producing higher-quality prints, but file sizes tend to remain large and so use up more storage space.

RAW

The third most commonly used format is RAW; the file extension differs depending on the manufacturer. Canon use the file extension '.CR2', for example, while Nikon use '.NEF'. Other manufacturers will have their own extension names, but basically they're all RAW. These files comprise solely the unprocessed data recorded by the camera's sensor. The benefit of using this format is that editing RAW files in today's sophisticated image-editing programs gives you greater control over adjustments to colour, contrast, brightness levels, sharpening, tone and so on. In addition, you'll also have all the raw, untouched image data to play around with, which usually provides much more detail, particularly in areas of shadow or highlights, than compressed JPEG files. For this reason, you should only use RAW if you intend to edit your images on a computer. Once edited, RAW files can usually be saved as TIFFs or high-quality JPEGs.

Memory cards

All cameras have memory cards. These come in a variety of shapes and sizes depending on the make and model, but all have storage space measured in megabytes (MB) or gigabytes (GB). If you're buying a digital camera for the first time, it's probably wise to invest in a memory card that is capable of storing more images than the one that will have been provided with the camera, so you're less likely to run out of storage space before having to download the images.

Camera Phones and Compact Cameras

Imaging sensors have come a long way in the last few years. Several years ago, few digital cameras boasted sensors with more than a million pixels, whereas today, mobile phones with 3MP cameras are commonplace, and many of today's compact cameras feature 10MP sensors or more.

Camera phones

From a purely photographic point of view, camera phones have some major disadvantages. The lenses are usually wide angle and fixed-focus, so they're designed to capture a broad view and make sure as much of the scene as possible is in focus. Although this helps ensure you'll get sharp images, there's clearly very little creative control. If you want to 'zoom' in, you have to move closer to the subject, and you cannot selectively control which parts of the image are in and out of focus. In addition, the sensors in a camera phone have to be very small, leading to 'noisy' images.

Setting these disadvantages to one side, however, a camera phone's portability, ease of use, and the fact that many people carry a camera phone with them at all times, encourages the taking of pictures. And as technology advances yet further – there are camera phones with 10MP sensors and 3x optical zooms – increasingly impressive photographic results will become attainable.

Compact cameras

A step further up the photographic ladder from camera phones is the plethora of compact digital cameras currently on the market. These vary from the inexpensive, 'entry-level' models to the feature-packed, high-specification and relatively expensive 'super' compacts. Basic compacts usually have a simple 3x optical zoom and are unlikely to have a separate viewfinder or a manual focus setting. They provide a few standard shooting modes, such as 'sport', 'landscape' and 'portrait'. However, even in the

▼ **BELOW** Most people now have a camera phone. They have their advantages, although one of the main problems is their tiny sensors and fixed lenses.

hands of someone with almost no photographic experience, most basic 'point-and-shoot' cameras are capable of producing very good-quality holiday photographs that can be printed up to postcard size.

At the other end of the spectrum, there are compacts that feature 12MP sensors, 15x optical zoom, a vast array of shooting modes, manual override, continuous shooting (allowing you to take between three and five images per second), image stabilization, and so on. In the right hands, and with favourable conditions, these super compacts are capable of producing photographs that are comparable to those of many digital SLRs.

Noise, dynamic range and response time

There are, however, some definite drawbacks to compact cameras, no matter how much they cost. The first is the perennial problem of noise. There's no getting away from the fact that, in many conditions, noise will be more apparent in images created by small sensors with small photosites, and all compact cameras will, by their nature, have small sensors and small photosites.

The second issue with smaller sensors is their narrow dynamic range – their ability to record detail in areas of shadow or highlight. Compared with larger sensors, small sensors will tend to make more shadow areas black, and more highlight areas white.

The final drawback can be most noticeable to photographers moving from film to digital compacts. The first thing many people notice is the time it takes for the digital compact camera to actually take the picture once the shutter button has been pressed. Known as 'shutter lag',

camera lens

LCD Screen

camera controls

shutter release

zoom

flash

LCD screen   macro mode   lens

▲ **ABOVE** Mid-range level compacts, such as this waterproof model with an inbuilt flash, are great for taking holiday snaps.

the delay is caused by the camera focusing, setting the correct exposure, and then 'charging' the sensor in preparation for capturing the image. In some entry-level compacts this can take up to 0.5 seconds – often long enough to miss a great shot, especially if it is a person's expression or pose.

Convenience

On the other hand, many of the more advanced compacts exhibit very little lag, produce good-quality A4 or even larger prints and provide the

▼ **BELOW** 'Superzoom' digital compacts offer a long zoom range and controls similar to those found on a dSLR.

more experienced photographer with sufficient manual control for more creative images. In addition, many compact cameras are able to shoot bursts of relatively high-quality video with sound. These features, combined with their relatively low cost and the fact that most people want to pop a camera in their pocket rather than

carry a bagful of equipment, are the reasons why more compacts are sold than any other type of digital camera.

Before choosing a model, think about your photographic needs. A dSLR is overkill for fun, quick holiday snaps and may attract unwanted attention; a compact, though, is unlikely to give stunning A3 landscapes.

Zoom lenses

A compact camera's zoom lens is usually described as being 3x, 5x or 10x. For a 5x zoom, this means an object will appear five times larger when the lens is set at its maximum setting than when it appears at its widest setting. Digital SLR zoom lenses are described using focal length – from a wide-angle setting (e.g. 35mm) to a telephoto setting (e.g. 105mm). You may also see an impressive-looking 'digital zoom' figure, but since the zoom is artificially created by the camera's software, it's best to ignore this as, in general, the more digital zoom you use, the more you degrade the final image.

mode dial   flash   direct print button   hotshoe   zoom control   mode dial

shutter release   focus assist lamp

focal length   lens   LCD screen   ISO control   exposure control

Bridge and Digital SLR Cameras

The next two categories of camera we'll look at are so-called 'bridge' cameras and digital single lens reflex cameras (dSLRs). It's easy to distinguish a dSLR from any other type of digital camera (see page 21), but differentiating between today's 'super zoom' compacts and bridge cameras is getting harder due to technological advances. Detailed here are some of the key differences.

Bridge cameras

All bridge, hybrid or 'prosumer' cameras, as they are also known, resemble dSLRs in several respects. So called because they 'bridge' the wide gap between compacts and dSLRs, bridge cameras are much larger than compacts and, in terms of shape, they can easily be mistaken for a dSLR.

Fixed lens

One of the key differences between bridge cameras and dSLRs is that the lens on a bridge camera is fixed, and so is not interchangeable. For this reason, most bridge cameras have powerful zoom lenses of 10x (30–300mm equivalent) to 15x (30–450mm) so that most shooting opportunities are catered for, from wide-angle landscapes to close-up sport or nature photography.

Manual control

Most bridge cameras offer a good level of manual control, from manual focusing to complete manual exposure. This provides greater creativity and encourages experimentation. In addition, bridge cameras respond almost as quickly as dSLRs and behave very much like them when in use. Unlike dSLRs, most bridge cameras can also shoot video clips.

Electronic viewfinders

Most bridge cameras have electronic viewfinders (EVFs), that relay exactly what the camera's lens is focusing on and framing – in fact, EVFs display exactly the same view as that shown by the camera's liquid crystal display (commonly abbreviated to LCD). In this way, EVFs behave more like a dSLR's viewfinder, except that there is a slight delay as the image is digitized and relayed to the viewfinder.

With similar controls, response times and functionality to a dSLR, but with only one lens to carry around (and usually costing less than most dSLRs) why not opt for a bridge model? Well, it's the same issue again – sensor size and noise. Bridge cameras are usually fitted with similar-sized sensors to those found in the higher spec compacts – around 8 x 6mm, compared to most dSLRs, which feature 22 x 16mm or larger sensors.

However, like many compacts, bridge cameras are able to produce excellent prints of between A4 and A3 in size, offer good levels of manual control for creative photography and, for many, are the ideal solution for their photographic needs.

viewfinder
mode dial
on/off switch
LCD screen
control pad
exposure compensation (EV)
image playback

BELOW Fujifilm's S5700/S700 is a popular dSLR-like camera featuring a 10x optical zoom lens.

pop-up flash
shutter release
focus assist light
10x zoom lens

Digital Single Lens Reflex

The dSLR market is the fastest growing of all the camera types – due to the fact that the cost of a basic dSLR has fallen dramatically in recent years. The least expensive dSLRs cost the same or, in some cases, even less than the more expensive compacts.

The key differences between dSLRs and other popular types of digital camera are the ability to change lenses, bright, 'instant' viewfinders, large sensors and negligible shutter lag.

Lenses

Being able to use lenses of different focal lengths, such as 10–20mm wide-angle zooms, 100–300mm telephoto zooms or even fixed length lenses such as a 60mm macro lens, allows you to use the same camera body for extreme wide-angle landscape or interior shots, and for close-up action sports or nature photography. Lenses vary enormously in quality and price, and owning a dSLR body allows you to build up a selection of good-quality lenses that will resolve more detail than the 'mega-zoom' lenses that are trying to cover both wide angle and telephoto.

Instant viewfinders

All dSLRs have instant and bright viewfinders. This is because the light from the scene passes through the lens via a mirror set at $45°$ and then through a prism and out through the view-finder. Thanks to this configuration of mirrors and prisms, the viewer is seeing exactly what the sensor will be exposed to when the mirror flaps up as the shutter release button is depressed to take the photo. This allows for more accurate framing and

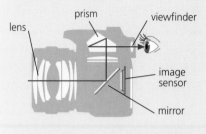

REFLEX VIEW

The term 'SLR' stands for 'single lens reflex' and refers to the camera's viewfinder system of a mirror and prism that allows you to look through the lens to compose your photographs. Essentially, this means that what you see in the viewfinder is what you get in the final picture.

Light (red) passing through a dSLR

easier composition, particularly in poor light, when electronic view-finders have trouble relaying a dark scene and also suffer from a slight lag.

Sensor size and shutter lag

At the risk of labouring the point, the large sensors used in all dSLRs provide almost noise-free images up to ISO settings of 400 or even 800. Even at ultra-high ISO settings such as 1600, when viewed at normal viewing distances, noise is often difficult to detect. Having the option to use a much wider range of ISO settings allows the photographer to try a greater variety of exposure settings and experiment with depth of field (see pages 82–89) and other creative techniques. Also, dSLRs do not suffer from noticeable shutter lag, making it easier to catch fast-moving action.

Being able to use high-quality lenses along with large sensors results in extremely high-quality images, even at A3 print sizes and beyond. If you want the best possible images and intend to photograph a variety of subjects in various shooting conditions, a dSLR with a selection of lenses is far and away the best option, especially in light of decreasing prices.

RIGHT AND BELOW With its large sensor and interchangeable lenses, a dSLR is the best option if you want to take high-quality photographs of a wide range of subjects in a wide range of conditions.

focus assist

focal length

hotshoe

flash button

lens release

zoom ring

viewfinder

prism

focus lock

image playback

LCD screen

control pad

The Camera Lens

Since the advent of digital cameras, manufacturers – and to a certain degree, camera magazines and websites – have been preoccupied with the performance of the cameras' internal components, especially the sensors and pixel count. Anyone new to digital photography could be forgiven for thinking that picture quality was ultimately down to the number of pixels crammed on to the imaging chip. In many ways this is unsurprising given the relative novelty of the technology and the amount of money spent on research and development in that specific area of digital imaging.

However, more experienced photographers are aware that the obsession with pixel count is something of a red herring. While sensors are a big piece of a camera's jigsaw puzzle – they are the part of the camera that records the image, and it's vital that they can record as wide a dynamic range as smoothly as possible – many would argue that the lens that gathers the light information in the first place is equally as important, if not more so.

ABOVE This fixed 35mm lens would be a wide-angle lens in a 35mm film camera or 'full frame sensor' dSLR. However, because sensors are smaller in most dSLRs the effective focal length is around 50mm.

Lens technology

Although it would be difficult to argue that lenses have undergone a similar revolution to camera bodies, huge amounts of money have been spent on developing lens technology. At the turn of the century, if you said you could produce a lens that covered a zoom range of 28–300mm, weighed less than 1.1lb (500g), produced acceptable results throughout its focal length range and had the ability to

ABOVE Macro lenses have the ability to focus extremely close to objects and so provide a greatly magnified image. True macro lenses have a ratio of 1:1 (1:1 will be printed on the lens barrel).

focus within 1.6ft (0.5m) to boot, no one would have taken you seriously – yet such lenses now exist.

Modern lenses are lighter, sharper, focus faster and are less prone to flare than ever before. Throw in the fact that many now have image stabilization (or vibration reduction) systems that allow you to hand hold a camera using shutter speeds as low as $^1/_{15}$ sec and still obtain sharp images, and it would be fair to say

Aperture range

A lens's maximum aperture is usually printed either on the barrel or the front of the lens. For example, a lens with a maximum aperture of f/2.8 will feature the figures 1:2.8. For zoom lenses, an aperture range is often provided, such as 1:4–5.6. This indicates that at the shorter focal length, such as 70mm for example, the aperture will open up to f/4, while at the longer focal length of the zoom, such as 300mm, the maximum aperture is reduced to f/5.6. These figures are important as they

indicate how 'fast' the lens is – the wider the possible aperture, the faster the lens. In other words, given the same lighting conditions a lens with a maximum aperture of f/2.8 will allow faster shutter speeds to be used, while still obtaining a correct exposure, than a 'slower' f/4 lens. The faster the lens the greater the creative control the photographer has, as it allows for a greater number of shutter/aperture exposure combinations, in turn resulting in greater control over depth of field and the shutter speed (see pages 76–77).

ABOVE This zoom lens has a wide aperture setting ranging from f/3.5 to f/6.5.

that photographers have never had it so good. Inevitably however, such technology does come at a price. There are lenses on the market today that cost the combined equivalent of a decent compact camera, printer, computer and all the software that is needed to edit images.

▶ **RIGHT** There are numerous types of zoom lens available for dSLRs. This 70–200mm zoom lens from Canon has the ability to zoom 3x.

OPTICAL LENS ELEMENTS

All lenses, whether interchangeable SLR lenses or those fixed to compact or hybrid cameras, are made up of a series of individual lenses known as 'elements'. Elements are one of either two types – diverging or converging. Both types of element exploit the fact that as light passes through glass (or clear plastic) with non-parallel sides, it will change direction. In a converging lens, the light will bend more at the thinner (top and bottom) parts of the lens than it does toward the thicker centre. This way the image converges to a point (known as the focal point) at some distance from the lens, and, if left, will continue to form an upside down image on any surface, such as an imaging sensor.

However, because of the optical aberrations that result from a single converging lens, a camera's lens employs a series of diverging and converging elements to try and correct these aberrations as far as possible. Other elements are also used to alter the focal length of a lens.

The number and exact shape of the elements in a camera lens, together with the space between each element and the type of glass or plastic used in their manufacture, are determined by the lens designer, who will use a computer to ensure that all the measurements are as precise as possible. The glass components are ground and polished and any plastic elements moulded to

extremely fine tolerances before being coated with anti-reflective materials. They are then assembled in the lens barrel together with the iris diaphragm (which controls the aperture), all of which are then optically aligned.

The overall construction must allow the optical elements to move in a controlled way so that the lens can focus accurately and consistently and, if necessary, allow a change in focal length in the case of zoom lenses. When you consider the fine tolerances and precise engineering used to create a lens and take into account that it must be strong enough to withstand minor knocks, it's not surprising that it can cost a great deal of money.

Typical lens array for a standard SLR lens

Light passing through a convex lens (top) and concave lens (bottom)

Choosing Lenses

The quality of any camera's lens will ultimately affect the overall image quality, yet all too often we overlook one of the most important elements of a camera system.

Compact and hybrid cameras

If you're looking to buy a compact or hybrid camera, or intending to upgrade your existing one, make sure you find out as much as you can about the quality of the lens. Many such cameras come fitted with 'superzooms', offering as much as 12x magnification (equivalent focal length 28–330mm). This is a big zoom, and the lens is unlikely to perform equally as well throughout the range. If you can, find out at what focal lengths the lens performs best, and see if that fits in with your photographic interests. If sports photography is your passion and you need to get close to the action, make sure the lens performs well at longer focal lengths. By contrast, if you're more interested in landscapes, you should ensure that the shorter focal length settings are its strong point.

▼ **BELOW** A diagram to show how moving the position of the same three lens elements can modify the path of light through a zoom lens.

24–105mm lens

14mm lens

Alternatively, consider whether you need such a long zoom in the first place. Tempting as the figures are, a 3x (28–85mm) or 5x (28–140mm) lens may be perfectly adequate for your needs, in which case you may find a camera that, although featuring a lens with a smaller range, has superior quality glass and performance. As always, before spending large amounts of money on camera equipment, do as much research as you can. There are plenty of excellent magazines and websites that exist offering unbiased advice.

dSLRs

For those of you who have made the leap to a dSLR, the issue of lenses is much more complicated – and, unfortunately, more expensive. One of the great advantages of a dSLR is that the lenses are interchangeable and usually provide excellent image quality. On the one hand, this is a good thing, as it allows access to a vast variety of lenses, with focal lengths ranging from around 10mm to 500mm (even 1200mm lenses are available). The downside is that the choice (and prices) can be bewildering.

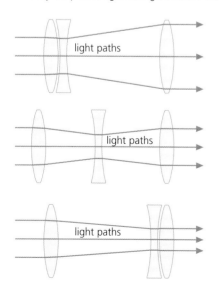

Zoom: digital versus optical

Some digital cameras boast an optical as well as a digital zoom, and the figures are often combined to make the camera's overall zoom capability sound very impressive. However, be cautious, as there is a distinct difference between an optical and digital zoom. When you use the optical zoom, the lens actually magnifies the image that is captured by the sensor; so as long as the lens performs well the image will be well defined. Digital zoom works by zooming in on the actual pixels already captured by the camera. So, although you're still magnifying the image, the camera is only magnifying the size of the pixels, which will usually lead to a fuzzy, degraded image. Avoid using digital zoom if you can.

55–200mm lens

Zoom versus prime

One of the big questions for SLR owners used to be whether to buy zoom or 'prime' lenses (lenses with a fixed focal length). While zooms offered much greater flexibility, primes were far superior in terms of image quality. However, the general improvement in lens technology, construction and components in recent years has seen a great leap in the image quality offered by zoom lenses, to the point where their convenience outweighs issues of quality.

The one area in which primes do still outclass zooms is their speed. Prime lenses are typically much faster (have a wider maximum aperture) than zooms, and so offer greater creative control. On the whole, however, improved high ISO performance and image stabilization do mean that you get better value for your money with zooms than a series of primes. With two good-quality zoom lenses covering, say, 24–70mm and 70mm–300mm equivalent focal lengths (efl), you'll have most photographic situations covered from wide-angle landscapes to telephoto sports.

Upgrading

With camera technology seeming to move so fast these days, it's tempting to save up and upgrade your camera as soon as the latest version becomes available. But before doing so, take a long look at the supposed benefits. They may be an additional megapixel or two (which doesn't translate to much), or more program settings (which you may never use), in which case, consider investing the money in a new lens instead. Perhaps you could increase the focal range of your system by buying a really wide-angle

▲ **ABOVE** The professional quality lens features image stabilization to help reduce camera shake. Tiny gyros in the lens are able to sense movement and move one of the lens elements to counter it.

lens. A wide-angle lens (such as efl 15–20mm) opens up all sorts of new compositional opportunities.

Alternatively, if you're happy with your range of focal lengths, trade in an existing lens and buy a higher-quality version – you'll notice a bigger improvement in image quality than with a slightly modified camera.

TELECONVERTERS

One way to add focal length to an existing lens is to fit a teleconverter. These effectively increase the focal length of the lens to which they're attached. Teleconverters are available for some makes of compact camera and screw on to the end of the lens, while others are designed for interchangeable lenses and sit between the dSLR body and the lens. The amount of magnification provided by a teleconverter depends on the specific type, but generally they provide a magnification of between 1.4x and 3x. These optical devices can be a less expensive way of increasing focal length, but can slow down the camera's autofocus system and reduce the maximum aperture setting of the lens.

Canon teleconverter

Nikon teleconverter

Basic Shooting and Composition

Having learned about the anatomy of a digital image, and the location of the main controls on your camera, it really pays to gain a good understanding of what these controls do to make the most of your photographic equipment. It may be tempting to leave the camera on fully automatic, but if you spend some time experimenting with the settings, you'll quickly see an improvement in the quality of your images. In this chapter, you'll find some basic tips and hints on composition – these are intended to act as pointers to help you start to think in visual terms and to find your own unique style.

Holding a Camera

Whether you own a small compact or are shooting with a dSLR fitted with a long telephoto lens, holding and supporting the camera properly will help to prevent camera shake.

Ultra compacts

Many 'ultra' compact-style digital cameras offer an LCD screen on the back of the camera to help you compose pictures. However, to use the screen, the camera has to be held away from the body, which can contribute to camera shake. In addition, many 'ultra' compacts are often smaller than the palm of your hand. People with larger hands sometimes hold the camera with the very tips of their fingers to avoid covering the lens. Although understandable, this can lead to camera shake as well.

Compacts

For compacts with a viewfinder, it's recommended that you use the viewfinder wherever possible. This will conserve power, help you keep the camera steady, and, in bright, sunny conditions, you will have a better chance of seeing the subject. The only time you really need to use the screen to compose a shot is when taking a close-up, as the offset viewfinder shows a somewhat different view to the one the lens is actually 'seeing'. This can lead to the subject being photographed slightly off-centre.

Digital SLR and bridge cameras

For those not used to a dSLR, its size and weight may come as a surprise. However, it's these aspects of dSLRs that make them stable and easier to hold steadily.

Many bridge cameras have a similar layout, with a long lens centred in the camera body, so much of the advice for holding a dSLR applies to bridge cameras. However, many such cameras are slightly smaller and lighter than a true dSLR.

Shutter release

Whatever type of camera you're using, avoid 'stabbing' the shutter release button. Instead, gently squeeze the shutter release button until the camera takes the photo.

Just before you capture the image, it also helps if you breathe in slightly and hold your breath. This will stop your chest moving up and down, which can potentially cause the camera to move just as you're taking the shot, which may well result in a blurred or out-of-focus photograph.

ABOVE Some ultra compact cameras don't have viewfinders and are very narrow and small. The best way to support such cameras is with both thumbs resting on the base of the camera, and both index fingers on the top.

ABOVE To keep the camera steady, use most of both fingers and thumbs, not just the tips. Also note how the remaining fingers are folded into the palms to avoid getting in the way of the camera's lens or flash unit.

ABOVE If you're using a compact without a viewfinder, avoid holding the camera with both arms outstretched, as this increases the risk of camera shake. For a more stable position, tuck your elbows into your body.

Landscape grip

Portrait grip

Lower-angle grip

Alternative lower-angle grip

▲ **ABOVE** Viewfinder compacts are bulkier than ultra compacts, allowing you to grip the camera with all the fingers of the right hand. Keep the fingers of the left hand clear to avoid them wandering in front of the lens.

▲ **ABOVE** When turning the camera 90° to take a portrait shot, grip the top of the camera with the right hand, which will also be used to press the shutter release button. Support the bottom of the camera with the left hand.

▲ **ABOVE** When taking a shot from a lower angle, don't just crouch down, or you'll run a high risk of camera shake. If the ground is dry, sit down cross-legged and rest the part of your arm just above the elbows on your knees.

▲ **ABOVE** If the ground is too wet to sit on, kneel on one knee and rest your arm on your knee. Don't rest your elbow directly on your knee as you'll end up with bone contacting bone which is likely to cause camera shake.

Digital SLR lenses

The lens of a dSLR plays a key role in how you handle the camera. The left-hand base of the camera should rest against the fleshy part of the left palm beneath the thumb. Wrap one, two or three fingers of the left hand around the barrel of the lens, depending on its length and how comfortable you feel, to support the camera/lens, manipulate the focus and, if using a zoom lens, the zoom ring. In this way you can frame, compose and focus the shot without taking your eye away from the view-finder, while your left hand makes adjustments to the camera settings.

HANDLING A TELEPHOTO LENS

With a long telephoto zoom lens attached, the position of the hands is much the same as when using a shorter focal length. However, depending on the length of the lens, the camera may feel more balanced and stable if the entire left hand is used to support the lens, with only the right hand supporting the camera body.

With longer lenses, it's also a good idea to support yourself against a wall, or try kneeling or even lying on the ground to give yourself a little extra stability. This is especially important when using long focal length lenses. As well as holding the camera safely and steadily, it's also important to ensure that you use an appropriate shutter speed for the focal length of the lens, as this will also help you avoid camera shake.

Shooting Stills with a Video Recorder

While many users will find it convenient to be able to shoot stills and video with the same compact device – so eliminating the need to carry separate units – there's a major disadvantage to using a camcorder for stills photography rather than a stills camera. The resolution of a video picture in 4:3 aspect ratio at standard definition is 720 x 576 pixels for the PAL system (common in Europe, Australia and several African countries), and 720 x 480 pixels where the NTSC system is used (in North America, Japan and many South American countries). Shooting and saving images to tape at these resolutions would generate images of less than 0.5 megapixels (MP) – equating to an image size of around $3^{1}/_{2}$ x $2^{1}/_{2}$in (9 x 6cm) – in other words vastly inferior to those achieved by even low-cost compact cameras.

Storage capacity

For a long while now, manufacturers have been including flash memory card slots in camcorder designs, such as Sony's Memory Stick and, more commonly, Secure Digital cards. Thanks to potential storage capacities of 16 gigabytes (GB), such cameras can store huge numbers of images at slightly higher resolution – typically 3MP – thanks to the incorporation of larger CCD and CMOS image sensors in newer camcorders. Since video doesn't require the use of very high-resolution image sensors to resolve even high-definition (HD)

▶ **RIGHT** Canon's HG10 high-definition camcorder features a 40GB internal hard drive, which records around 5½ hours of footage, although the 3-megapixel stills the camera can capture can only be stored on a memory card.

video, manufacturers tend not to include anything above 3MP sensors in their products. Even so, at these resolutions, good-quality A4 prints are achievable. Where a camcorder is advertised as possessing a CCD or CMOS sensor capable of generating more pixels than a 4:3 or widescreen 16:9 ratio video picture needs, it's often to facilitate extra features such as EIS (Electronic Image Stabilization) or digital stills with higher resolution than their equivalent video frames. The camcorder can't use any more than the video picture requires, so the larger sensor array would be largely redundant.

▲ **ABOVE** Despite its small size, Panasonic's HDC-SD5 camcorder is a high-definition (HD) model, capable of capturing video and still images at 1,920 x 1,080 pixels, or 2.07MP.

Image sensors

As with digital stills cameras, the effective resolution of an image is related to the size of the image sensor. Although $^{1}/_{3}$in CCDs and CMOS sensors aren't that uncommon in stills cameras, it's more likely that today's low-cost camcorder will use a sensor size of only $^{1}/_{4}$in or, even more commonly, $^{1}/_{6}$in. Smaller CCDs typically generate smaller pixels, too, so camcorders that employ three CCDs

RIGHT This image measures 1,920 x 1,080 pixels and was grabbed from a frame of high-definition video using Panasonic's solid-state HDC-SD5 AVCHD camcorder, which benefits from optical image stabilization, from a shooting distance of approximately 20ft (6m). As you can see, the definition is much better than that of Standard video.

have distinct benefits in that each CCD can be assigned the job of processing one of the three red, green and blue primary colours. Three CCDs really are better than one.

High-definition video

More recently there has been an increase in the number of camcorders designed to facilitate HD video production. Unlike the standard-definition (SD) video pictures we have grown accustomed to over the years, HD brings to video a substantial increase in the potential number of pixels available when generating images. The standard internationally recognized resolution for HD television and video is 1,920 horizontal pixels by 1,080 vertical pixels. While for video users, that's a massive increase in resolution designed to produce superb video images, it's still low even for those digital photographers working on a budget. However, flat screen LCD and plasma TV displays benefit from progressive scan, which produces a smoother, more detailed, image. For that reason we'll soon see a sharp increase in camcorders that make use of it.

Shooting photographic stills

To shoot stills with a camcorder is as simple as pressing the Photo button. Usually this will override any movie functions – unless it's possible to shoot stills and movies simultaneously. Many camcorders now feature a mechanical shutter that prevents blurred images when the shot is taken. Images can either be downloaded to a computer via USB connection or by inserting the memory card into a separate reader.

Most camcorders enable you to switch between Auto and Manual modes, which means that you can take control of things like focus, aperture, white balance and even shutter speed. Although a PAL standard TV will scan at 25 fps (frames per second) – the equivalent of $^1/_{25}$ sec – a camcorder can electronically emulate faster and slower shutter speeds so that speeds the equivalent of $^1/_{2000}$ sec are possible. Several models – especially those from Canon – will automatically calculate shutter speed depending on the selected aperture (the equivalent of Aperture priority), and vice versa. The majority of low- and medium- cost

camcorders offer an optical zoom ratio of between 10x and 20x, although it's not uncommon to see digital zoom ratios of 800x and even 1,000x. Use of these should be avoided due to the heavy pixellation and blockiness they produce. Careful use of the zoom can produce good stills, especially when used in conjunction with image stabilization – but always use a tripod or other means of support when possible. Zooms are just one of the features that are better on camcorders than on many compact stills cameras, and the larger adjustable LCD screens provide greater flexibility when shooting and playing back material.

RIGHT
An increasing number of camcorders can be connected directly to a printer.

Automatic Shooting Modes

All digital cameras, from an entry-level point-and-shoot compact to a professional dSLR, have a variety of auto or preset shooting modes. These modes, such as 'Portrait', 'Landscape' or 'Sports', indicate the type of image or the conditions in which the photograph is being taken and allow the camera to decide on the most appropriate settings. These differ from the semi-automatic or manual modes, which determine how much and the type of manual control the photographer has over the camera.

Common preset modes

The number and specific type of preset or automatic modes that a camera has vary depending on the make and model, but just about all will feature the modes listed below. The icons indicating the modes will also vary, so if you're unsure about which icon represents which mode, look in the camera's manual.

 Auto
As the name suggests, in Auto mode everything is automatic, with the camera taking complete control of all the settings. It will set the ISO, white balance and focusing mode, then focus the lens, assess light

Close-up/Macro mode

Beach/Snow mode

Portrait mode

levels and set an appropriate exposure, plus fire the flash if necessary. This mode is often used by beginners or those unfamiliar with a new camera as it almost guarantees a correctly exposed and sharp image.

 Close-up/Macro
The Close-up or Macro mode is used to take close-up pictures of small subjects such as flowers or insects. How close you can get to the subject depends on the camera and lens, but with most compacts it will be between $2/3$–6in (2–15cm). The depth of field at this small distance is very narrow (see pages 86–87), making it difficult to keep everything in focus. This can often result in effective, creative shots where only the centre part of a flower is in focus, for example. However, if you want the entire subject to be in focus,

you should shoot from directly above (or directly below) the subject so as much of the subject as possible is at the same distance from the lens.

Portrait
In this mode, the camera will set the largest possible aperture (smallest number) to create a narrow

Panorama/Stitch mode

depth of field. This throws the background out of focus so that more emphasis is placed on the subject's face.

Landscape

This mode works in the opposite way to Portrait. The camera will set the smallest possible aperture (highest number) to create the widest possible depth of field. This ensures that as much of the scene – and ideally from foreground to background – is in focus.

Sports/Action

When photographing any fast-moving sport or action scene – such as football or motor racing – select the Sports (or Action) mode. In this mode, the camera will automatically select the fastest possible shutter speed (depending on the available light) in order to 'freeze' the action. You'll usually have better success if you follow, or pan, the subject through the lens for a few seconds before taking the shot. If the camera has a variety of focusing modes then it will usually select 'continuous focus' and also 'continuous shooting' if that's another option.

Night Portrait

The Night Portrait mode is designed for taking photographs of people outside during the evening or at night. The camera will set a relatively long shutter speed to ensure that the dark background is captured, while firing the flash to light and 'freeze' the subject. This is known as 'slow sync'. You should always make sure that your subject remains still – even after the flash has fired – as the camera may still be recording, albeit only for a fraction of a second.

Movie

Most recent compacts and bridge cameras have the ability to record video with sound. Although the quality of image and sound won't be as good as a dedicated video camera,

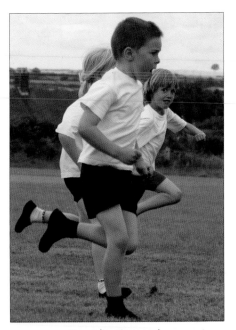

Sports/Action mode

for many people the option to record short video clips is important. Be aware, however, that recording video will use up a great deal of space on the memory card.

Other preset modes

Other common modes that appear on many digital cameras include:

Beach/Snow

Both these modes will ensure the camera accurately exposes images in conditions where you are faced with bright ambient light.

Panorama/Stitch

In this mode, after the first image of a prospective panorama is taken, the exposure and white balance

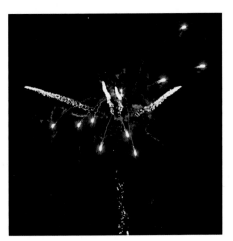

Fireworks mode

are 'locked' so that all subsequent images have the same coloration, tone and contrast. You then pan the camera to the next section of the panorama and align the next image with the previous one, of which about a third appears semi-transparent on the LCD screen.

Fireworks

Using Fireworks mode the camera will deliberately select a slow shutter speed so that the trails from fireworks are captured.

Black and White

Numerous cameras, including some dSLRs, feature a Black and White mode, which allows you to shoot black and white or sepia-toned images. You can often achieve better results using image-editing software, but if you print directly from the memory card and want black and white images this mode is essential.

Black and White mode

Semi-automatic Shooting Modes

In addition to the main automatic shooting modes found on almost all compact cameras and most dSLRs, many other compacts and just about all dSLRs also feature a number of semi-automatic modes. These are usually Program (P), Shutter priority (S), which is also known as Time value (Tv), and Aperture priority (A), which is also known as Aperture value (Av). These modes offer much more creativity in that you have greater control over aperture and shutter speed selection, but at the same time they also help you to achieve an appropriate exposure. If your camera has these modes, it will also have a Manual (M) option, which we will look at later (see Understanding Exposure on pages 76–77).

Program (P)

Depending on the make and model of your camera, the Program (P) mode will usually behave in a similar way to the full Auto mode, in that the camera selects a suitable combination of aperture and shutter speed to achieve the correct exposure. However, selecting P will also allow you to change the ISO setting, image size and quality, the metering mode and a number of other settings that are set automatically when the camera is in Auto mode. In other words, while Program allows you to tailor certain settings, you'll generally produce correctly exposed pictures.

Program shift/Flexible program

Another way in which Program differs to Auto in most cameras is that while Program mode will automatically set an initial aperture/shutter speed combination, it will also allow you to change that combination. If, for example, you want a fast shutter

LEFT Most digital cameras, including dSLRs, support modes that are selectable either by a dial or a menu.

ABOVE With the camera in Program (P) mode, it will set an aperture/shutter speed combination that is appropriate for the amount of light available.

speed to freeze action, you can select a faster shutter speed using a control dial and the camera will automatically increase the size of the aperture (select a smaller number) so that you will still obtain a correct exposure. This is usually known as 'Program shift' or 'Flexible program'.

In a similar way, if you want to reduce the size of the aperture (select a higher number) in order to ensure that as much of the scene as possible is in focus, the camera will select a slower shutter speed to make sure that the image is still correctly exposed. With most cameras, if you select a aperture/shutter combination that will produce an under- or overexposed image, the camera is likely to provide either a visual or audible warning. Altering the ISO setting so that a correct combination of aperture and setting is made available can often be the solution to this.

▲ **ABOVE** This image was taken in Shutter priority/Time value mode, with a fast shutter speed ($^1/_{250}$ sec) selected manually to 'freeze' the movement of the water. The camera then automatically set an appropriate aperture (f/4.5) to ensure accurate exposure.

▲ **ABOVE** This image was also taken in Shutter priority/Time value mode, with a slow shutter speed ($^1/_6$ sec) deliberately chosen in order to capture the blurred movement of the flowing water. Again, the camera automatically set the aperture (f/22).

▲ **ABOVE** Both images were taken in Aperture priority/Aperture value mode. On the left, a wide aperture (f/4.0) gives a narrow depth of field and the camera automatically sets the shutter speed ($^1/_{1000}$ sec). On the right, a narrow aperture (f/22) is chosen resulting in a wide depth of field – the camera automatically set the shutter speed ($^1/_{50}$ sec).

▲ **ABOVE** Using the Program shift or Flexible program modes is a good way to begin experimenting with aperture and shutter speed combinations. In the top image, a fast shutter speed/wide aperture combination has 'frozen' the flowers, but because of the wide aperture (low number) some of the flowers are out of focus. In the lower image, the slow shutter speed/narrow aperture combination has resulted in an image that is sharply focused front to back, but the slow shutter speed has resulted in some blurry flowers as they were blown in the wind.

Shutter priority (S)/Time value (Tv)

In this mode you can set a specific shutter speed – fast to freeze action, or slow to deliberately blur people or objects. The camera will set an appropriate aperture depending on the available light. If the shutter speed is set too fast or too slow, the camera will either blink or beep to warn that the image will be incorrectly exposed, but the shutter will still fire in case the 'incorrect' exposure is deliberate. Or, you could alter the ISO to see if that produces an acceptable exposure.

Aperture priority (A)/Aperture value (Av)

This mode works in a similar way to the S/Tv mode, but the opposite way around. You can set a large aperture (small number) to throw a background out of focus, or set a small aperture (large number) to increase the depth of field (to ensure a landscape is in focus from foreground to background). The camera will automatically select an appropriate shutter speed to ensure a 'correct' exposure or warn you of an 'incorrect' exposure.

Autofocusing Modes

To make life easier for us, today's digital cameras have sophisticated autofocusing (AF) systems that help ensure our images are in focus while we can concentrate on composition or predicting someone's expression. Most AF systems in today's digital cameras are known as 'passive' autofocus and work in one of two ways.

Contrast measurement

This is the least complex AF system, which is used in entry-level compact cameras. It uses a simple sensor (as opposed to the camera's main image sensor) to detect at which point the lens produces an image with the highest level of contrasting pixels. This indicates the lens is sharply focused – an in-focus black and white stripe will have higher contrasting pixels than an out-of-focus stripe, which will appear more grey.

Phase detection

This more complex AF system is used on sophisticated compacts and most dSLRs. Known as 'phase detection', light from the scene is split into two from different parts of the lens. These parts are compared by the AF sensor, which will then direct the AF servos (tiny electrical motors) to make adjustments to the lens, depending on the similarity in light patterns between the two images.

Under most conditions both systems work well and can provide fast, accurate focus. However, if the light is poor, or the scene exhibits little contrast (such as a blue sky or a repetitive pattern), you'll hear the camera's AF system 'hunting' as it tries to find the point of focus.

To combat the first situation, the camera will automatically 'fire' a rapid succession of light beams from an

AF (autofocus) points

Unlike most point-and-shoot cameras, which have a single autofocus (AF) point that will focus the lens only on the central part of the scene, the majority of dSLRs and some compact cameras have a number of selectable AF points placed around the viewfinder. These can be chosen individually (such as top left of the scene) or all at once. If an individual point is selected, the camera will use that point to focus on – which is useful if you're trying to focus on a particular part of a scene that is not in the centre of the viewfinder.

'AF assist lamp' so that the AF system can 'see'. If there is no AF assist lamp, most cameras will fire the flash. Where the scene is too uniform in tone and colour for the camera to accurately

▼ **BELOW** Many cameras feature a continuous AF system, which tracks the subject and keeps it constantly in focus. As soon as the shutter release is depressed, focus is locked and the picture taken.

▼ **BELOW** Occasionally, even continuous AF cannot keep up with the pace. Here, due to shutter lag, by the time the camera actually fired, the subject had moved too close to the camera to remain in focus.

△ **ABOVE** Advanced autofocus systems can track moving elements and predict where they will be at the exact moment the shutter fires. With 'predictive' or Artificial Intelligence focus, these racers are pin sharp.

△ **ABOVE** Less than a second later, predictive autofocus has accurately estimated the runners' positions, counteracting the slight delay between pushing the shutter release and the camera firing.

differentiate pixels, the quickest way to resolve this is to find something the camera can focus on that is the same distance away. Otherwise, if the camera has the option to switch to manual focus you can focus the lens yourself.

Single AF versus continuous AF

Many cameras have two AF settings – single AF and continuous AF. Single AF (also known as 'one-Shot'/'single-Shot') should be used when the subject is relatively still, such as landscapes or portraits. Pressing the shutter release halfway will set the focus, and the camera will go on to take a picture if it focuses and the shutter release is fully pressed. In continuous AF mode the camera focuses continuously, and only 'locks' onto the subject when the shutter release is pressed halfway. This makes a continuous AF mode useful for taking photos of moving subjects. The idea is to follow the subject through the viewfinder or on the rear LCD screen and the camera will try to keep it in focus until you want to take the photo. This mode is not without its problems. There is often a delay between pressing the shutter release and the camera taking the picture – and subjects in motion, by their very nature are moving – often resulting in images that will be out of focus.

Predictive AF

To combat such situations, some cameras (mostly dSLRs) incorporate a 'predictive' AF system. This mode works best when the subject is either moving toward or retreating from the camera at a constant rate. The camera's AF system will track the subject as it moves into the frame and attempt to predict where it will be at the precise moment the shutter fires. In effect, the camera is estimating the time it takes for the shutter release to be pressed and for a picture to be taken. In this way it helps to ensure the subject will remain in focus at the precise moment the exposure is made.

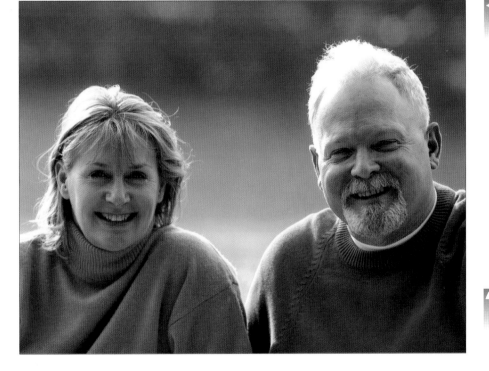

◁ **LEFT** For stationary subjects, 'single' autofocus is recommended. Depressing the shutter release halfway will lock the focus.

△ **ABOVE** These diagrams illustrate how some cameras rely on contrast to achieve focus. The in-focus lines (left) have greater contrast than the out-of-focus lines (right).

Metering Modes

In order to produce an image that is not too bright (overexposed) or too dark (underexposed), all digital cameras need a way to assess accurately how much light is present in the scene that is being photographed. Historically, photographers used handheld light meters to measure the amount of light falling onto the subject – in fact many professional studio photographers still use such devices to ensure they know precisely what the light levels are. However, with these 'incident' light meters, you need to be able to place the meter very close to the object being photographed to 'read' the light.

For most of us this is not usually practical, so modern cameras have built-in light meters that measure the light reflected from the subject or from the scene as a whole. However, because light levels can vary drastically – even within the same scene – many cameras provide a number of different ways to measure light to help you achieve the correct exposure. These are known as metering modes. There are three common metering modes, and all digital cameras will have at least one, while many will include all three.

Centre-weighted metering

This is the most commonly used metering system in digital cameras that do not offer any metering option, such as some compact cameras. In this mode, the metering is biased or weighted to the centre of the viewfinder and then averaged for the entire scene. The idea is that for most shots the subject of the image will be in the centre of the frame and therefore accurately exposed, while the rest of the scene is averaged out. If there is a big difference between the lightest and darkest parts of the image (such as land and sky), then the camera will attempt to find the most appropriate setting to ensure that most of the photograph is exposed as accurately as possible.

This mode is very useful when taking portrait shots, particularly if the subject is standing in front of a light background (this is referred to as backlighting). However, if the subject of the picture is off centre, or the background or foreground is extremely light or dark, they may well be incorrectly exposed.

Spot/partial metering

As its name suggests, spot or partial metering takes a reading only from the very centre spot of the viewfinder and sets an accurate exposure for that part of the image only – no readings are taken from any other part of the scene. True spot metering measures the central 1–2% of the viewfinder area, whereas partial metering will measure around 9–10% of the area. This metering mode should

RIGHT When set to centre-weighted, the camera sets an exposure that puts most emphasis on the central part of the image, but takes into account the rest of the scene; here the flower is slightly overexposed because of the dark leaves around it. The schematic diagram (far right) shows how centre-weighted metering assesses the scene.

RIGHT When set to spot or partial, the camera sets an exposure appropriate only for the central part of the scene. Here, the flower is accurately exposed and the surround underexposed. The diagram (far right) shows how the metering assesses the scene.

1. Individual light measurement is made in every segment of the scene to be shot.

2. The camera searches a database with light measurements from 50,000 characteristic subject situations.

3. After analysis, the optimal exposure values are calculated.

LEFT Put simply, in evaluative or matrix mode, the camera assesses the scene to be photographed and compares it with a database of many thousands of 'comparative' shots to work out the optimum exposure.

be used when the subject must be correctly exposed, no matter how much (or how little) light is falling on the surrounding areas, or during close-up photography. While this form of metering provides the most predictable results, if the area used to take the reading from does not provide the best average, the result will be unacceptably overexposed or underexposed. For this reason, spot or partial metering is often not available on many point-and-shoot cameras.

Evaluative/matrix metering

This is the most sophisticated of all the metering systems, and is the 'default' mode for most cameras that offer metering options. It works by taking multiple readings from various points in the scene, while also assessing the position of the main subject, foreground and background, overall brightness, any front- or backlighting, colour and so on. The camera then compares these readings with a database of tens of thousands of 'typical' photographic scenes and selects the exposure that most closely resembles one in its database. In other words, the camera guesses what type of picture is being taken, whether it's a landscape with a bright sky and dark land or a portrait at dusk. Most of the time, evaluative or matrix metering does a surprisingly good job at selecting the most appropriate exposure for any given scene, but it's by no means foolproof as it employs a certain amount of 'guesswork'. More experienced photographers often complain that they lose a certain amount of control when using evaluative metering.

Which mode is best?

Generally, if there are no marked differences in highlights and shadows, then evaluative or matrix metering is more likely to get the exposure right. If, however, there are distinct differences in light and dark areas, or if the subject is backlit, or you need to expose for a specific area of a scene, you will probably find that using either spot/partial or centre-weighted metering will serve you better.

LEFT The camera's matrix metering has accurately captured this scene, which contains bright highlights and dark shadows.

Histograms

Working digitally has a number of benefits, one of the most important being that the colour, brightness and tonal values of the individual pixels that make up the image are recorded as soon as the image is taken.

These values can be reviewed in two ways on the camera's LCD screen – firstly, as the image itself or secondly, as a graphic tonal representation which is known as a histogram.

Being able to interpret histograms will help you to assess whether or not your image has the acceptable tonal values that make for a well-exposed shot, particularly in bright sunlight when it's difficult to see clearly a review of the image on the camera's LCD screen.

Interpreting a histogram

A histogram can normally be called up on the LCD screen on the back of your camera when shooting or playing back images. It is a form of graph where the x- (horizontal) axis represents the entire digital tonal range from black to white (0–255), while the y- (vertical) axis represents the number of pixels with a specific tonal value.

It can be helpful to try to mentally divide the x-axis into three sections – shadows to the left, midtones in the middle and highlights to the right. An ideally exposed image would generate a symmetrical, humped-shape histogram that smoothes gently out to the black and white points at either end of the histogram. For less well-exposed examples, a histogram that features the majority of the pixels in the left part of the histogram would indicate an underexposed, or dark (low-key), image, while one in which most of the pixels were grouped to the right would suggest an overexposed, very light (high-key) image.

▲ **ABOVE** A snowy scene will produce a histogram that has a large number of pixels grouped to the highlight (right) end of the histogram. However, both ends of the histogram curve uniformly to both the black point (left) and the white point (right). This indicates a good range of tones from black to white.

▲ **ABOVE** Although exhibiting a number of individual peaks that represent specific regions of the image, such as buildings and mountain shadows, this image has produced an even histogram overall. Both ends drop gradually to the black and white points – indicative of a well-exposed image with a full tonal range.

▲ **ABOVE** This dark, reflective shot of a garden wall showing the garden beyond has resulted in a histogram with a grouping of pixels to the shadow (left) end of the histogram. But again, because the graph drops down to the base of the black point (albeit sharply) most of the shadow detail is discernible.

▲▼ **ABOVE AND RIGHT** The dark water in the background and the relatively dark subject have fooled the camera into overexposing the surf in this image. This is shown by the spike of pixels against the right-hand end of the histogram.

▲ **ABOVE** The boy's dark wetsuit has been underexposed in this image despite the relative lack of bright highlights. The spike of pixels at the black point of the histogram shows this and indicates that some shadow detail has been lost.

Clipped highlights/shadows

One of the most useful aspects of reviewing an image's histogram is that it will quickly alert you to any clipped highlights or shadows. Either of these can occur in a scene that exhibits a very wide tonal range – that is, an image that contains large areas of dark shadows and equally large areas of bright highlights. Depending on your specific camera and how its metering system works, in such a difficult lighting situation it's likely that the dark shadows will be underexposed and become entirely black with no discernible detail (clipped shadows) or the highlight areas will be overexposed and rendered entirely white (clipped highlights), or both. Bright areas of an image that are overexposed to the point at which they appear as pure white are often referred to as 'blown highlights'.

Both clipped shadows and clipped highlights are quickly detected on a histogram in the form of a large group

or distinct 'spike' of pixels stacked against either end of the histogram. If, when reviewing a histogram, you see that groups of pixels are pushed to either end of the histogram try recomposing the shot so that fewer bright areas or less shadows are visible in the frame.

Blown highlights are extremely intrusive and are usually impossible to remedy in photo-editing software as there's no information to start with. Detail can be far more easily extracted from dark shadows in editing software. For this reason, it's often better to ensure you get a more accurate

exposure for the lighter areas than for the darker ones, especially if you are using a compact camera. There are various techniques you can use to help you get the best possible results in difficult light situations and we'll cover these in the Manual Exposure section on pages 78–79.

▲▼ **ABOVE AND RIGHT** Unsurprisingly, this grey black and white image produces a fairly uniform histogram, apart from the peaks at either end created by dark shadows and bright highlights.

Colour Temperature and White Balance

While watching a glorious sunrise, enjoying a spectacular view at midday, or walking down an artificially lit street at night, our eyes and brain make adjustments so that in most circumstances we compensate for the possible variation in the colour of the light – to us a white sheet of paper looks white no matter where or when we look at it. However, this is misleading, and in order to get accurate colours from your camera, it's important to understand a little about how light can vary in colour.

Natural light

Colour, or light, temperature can be accurately measured using the Kelvin (°K) temperature scale. During the course of a day (depending on where you live and the time of year), the light temperature will vary and this affects the colour of the light. For example, at sunrise, the light will often take on a reddish hue and has a temperature of around 2,500°K.

As the sun rises higher in the sky the light becomes increasingly white, until around midday when the light reaches a temperature of around 5,500°K. At this temperature there is no noticeable colour bias, which is why flash units also use this neutral colour temperature.

As the sun begins to set, the colour temperature drops again, and the light will often return to the red colours apparent at sunrise.

Cloud cover (or a lack of it) can also affect the colour of light. For example, while a cloudy day has relatively neutral light of between 6,000°K and 7,000°K, a bright blue sky has a temperature of around 10,000°K. This will cast a noticeably blue light, which can make your pictures appear cool.

Artificial light

It's not just natural light that exhibits varying colour temperatures. Various types of artificial light also have different temperatures, and usually these are much more apparent than natural colour temperature shifts. For example, a standard 60-watt incandescent (tungsten) light bulb, the type used in a great many table lamps, will generate a colour temperature of around 3,000°K,

ABOVE These three shots were taken at different times of the day – sunrise, midday and sunset. The top image was taken at around 5:30am and the sunrise was uninterrupted by cloud. The red quality to the light is typical of a colour temperature of around 3,000°K. By comparison, the second image appears much more neutral in colour. However, by sunset (bottom image), the colour temperature returns to around 3,000°K, reintroducing the red glow that accompanied sunrise.

Auto white balance

Daylight

Cloudy

Shade

creating a warm, reddish light, while some fluorescent lights have relatively high temperatures of around 7,000°K, creating a cold, green-blue colour cast.

White balance

Traditionally, photographers used to use a variety of coloured filters attached to the camera's lens to counteract the effect of colour casts. If the light was too blue, they would use a red-coloured filter to 'warm-up' the image, and vice versa. While using filters on a digital camera that accepts them is certainly one way of correcting colour casts, many compacts won't take filters. However, all digital cameras have a white balance (WB) setting that does the same job.

Auto white balance (AWB)

All digital cameras have an auto white balance (AWB) setting. In simple terms, this works by making the brightest element in the image white and then, using that as a point of reference, adjusting all the other hues to create true-to-life colour. However, if there's no 'white' reference point, or the scene is dominated by one particular colour, the camera's AWB

setting can be tricked into making the wrong decision. To counteract this, your digital camera is likely to feature a number of preset white balance modes, including incandescent (tungsten), fluorescent, daylight, flash, cloudy and shade. These modes use a fixed temperature setting common to those specific lighting conditions and will usually produce more accurate colours than the AWB setting.

In addition, more feature-packed compacts and many dSLRs also feature a custom white balance setting. With this setting you shoot a white card under the lighting conditions in which you're working. The camera will record this as white and use that setting for all subsequent shots. Some cameras will also allow you to input the exact Kelvin setting if you know the colour temperature of the light source being used.

Quick correction

If your images appear too warm or red, selecting a higher temperature setting ('daylight' to 'cloudy' for example) and retaking the photo should give you more accurate colours.

Similarly, if the image appears too cool or blue, selecting a lower temperature setting will warm the image. Finally, although we usually strive to get an accurate white balance, correcting a wonderful sunset shot so that pinkish walls are accurately rendered as white would detract from the picture. This is an obvious case where we might want to retain the colour cast, as it adds atmosphere to the picture. Similarly, the sickly green of certain street lighting may be exactly what you're after to portray an urban environment so, for creative effect, try using the 'wrong' white balance and see what results you get.

Colour temperature

The average colour temperature in Kelvin for a variety of typical light sources:

Candle light	1,500°
Incandescent/tungsten	2,500°
Sunrise/sunset	3,000°
Midday sun/flash	5,500°
Overcast sky	6,500°
Hazy sky	8,000°
Blue sky	10,000°+

Composition

Having covered basic automatic and semi-automatic shooting, metering and focusing modes, it's time to look at some basic composition principles. Learning about the added creativity these can bring to the photographer will not only help you visualize how your pictures will turn out, but give them greater impact, too.

Good composition

Over the next few pages we'll be looking at various techniques that have been employed by artists and photographers over many years to improve composition. But what is good composition?

On one level, good composition is all about 'arranging' the elements in the viewfinder or on the LCD screen so that their shape, form, colour and tone interact with one another in a way that looks visually appealing. Of course this is very subjective – an image that resonates with one viewer may quite easily leave another cold. Employing certain compositional techniques, however, is usually a good place to start.

Capture the moment

For many new photographers, one of the hardest skills to learn is how to capture the complete essence of a moment or scene, just as we experienced it when taking the image. For example, if we're at the beach we have the added benefit of experiencing the smell and the sound of the seagulls squawking, the fine texture of sand and the heat of the sun – all of which formulate that very specific sense of time and place. Yet when we come to view our images on screen or in print we often find that they don't necessarily recreate the original sense of time and place.

Good composition is a way of using techniques that will help you create images that are visually pleasing and successfully conjure up the emotions and memories of a specific location or event. We're now going to examine a number of the basic rules of composition. However, it's important not to become preoccupied by these 'rules' as this can stifle creativity and hinder spontaneity, so consider these rules more as guidelines; something to help rather than struggle to adhere to.

▽ **BELOW** When faced with a seascape or landscape, most photographers will naturally use their camera in a horizontal, or 'landscape', orientation. But there is no rule that says you can't shoot an 'upright' image if the scene warrants it.

△ **ABOVE** The children in this picture aren't in the middle of the frame and there's a lot of background around them, but there is still no doubt that they are the focus of the photograph.

▽ **BELOW** The landscape form of this city shot captures the sweeping river front of Budapest, with its uniform rows of windows.

△ **ABOVE** By using a fast shutter speed, the girl in this image has been frozen, making it possible to clearly see her expression and capture the moment.

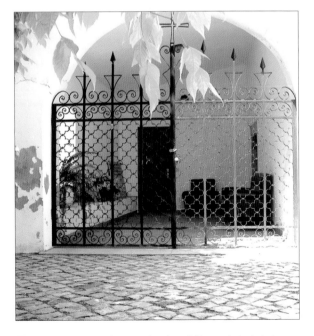

△ **ABOVE** Here the photographer has deliberately included some leaves in the top of the image. This is a form of 'framing' that adds depth to an image.

Finding inspiration

There will certainly be times when, as a photographer, you feel uninspired. Prolonged periods of poor weather or a sense that you have little in the way of subject matter will often bring on these periods. Joining a camera club is a good way of helping you through such moments. You'll meet like-minded people, be given specific photographic challenges and learn and share techniques that will improve your images.

Alternatively, join an on-line photographic community, such as Flickr (www.flickr.com). Most are free to join, have innumerable forums, and specific areas for certain subjects and styles of photography. They're also a fun way of getting feedback on your own images.

Fill the Frame

Of all the compositional rules and tips, perhaps the most effective (and straightforward to understand) is to 'fill the frame'. It's amazing how many photographs – especially portraits – are taken either from too far away or do not use the camera's zoom facility to its full potential.

Part of the reason for this is because our brains are excellent at 'filtering' out the sights and sounds that we're not specifically concentrating on. When we focus on something, it is that object that fills our 'mental frame' and has our undivided attention. In our mind's eye it appears to fill the frame even though we might physically be some distance away. This will almost certainly result in images that render the subject small and insignificant in the frame.

Optical proximity

Robert Capa, who was one of the greatest war photographers and one of the founders of *Life* magazine – once famously remarked that, "If your photos aren't good enough, you're not close enough". This is precisely what filling the frame is all about. Although at the time he said it, Capa was undoubtedly implying physical 'closeness' – and, of course, getting physically closer to your subject will certainly help fill the frame – with today's more sophisticated and superior lens technology, we can also get closer optically. Later on in the book, we'll be looking in more detail and focal lengths, and the impact a long focal length (or telephoto) lens has on an image, but for now, use your camera's zoom facility to get in close to your subject – you'll be amazed at the impact this can bring.

By filling the frame, you will not only reduce the risk of inadvertently including any distracting background or foreground clutter, but viewers will be left in no doubt about the subject of the photograph.

ABOVE AND RIGHT Our mind can play strange tricks on us when we're behind the camera. Because we're so 'focused' on the subject of a photograph, we're not always aware of the extraneous parts of the scene surrounding the subject. One good tip is to compose the image, then close your eyes and visualize the scene that you have just composed. When you open your eyes again you may be surprised to discover how different the reality is from the image you thought you were about to take in your 'mind's eye'. Always try to fill the frame with your chosen subject.

ABOVE Even something as mundane as a trailer window with two dish cloths can create an interesting, symmetrical composition if used to 'fill the frame' under favourable lighting conditions.

ABOVE Budapest's airport has some interesting geometrical shapes, patterns and lines that are difficult to capture in their entirety. After a while, the photographer stopped trying to capture the whole frontage and instead focused on the name and the structural elements that had first caught his attention.

RIGHT Here the photographer wanted to capture the wonderful purple of a species of flower growing on cliff tops. With the first image, the colour and quantity of the flowers is adequately captured, but including the beach and sea distracts the viewer from the subject – it's just not clear what exactly we're meant to be looking at. By filling the frame, the colour and abundance of the flowers are enhanced as they are the only subject in the frame with no added distractions.

Get in close

There are two ways of filling the frame for maximum impact and eradicating unwanted backgrounds:
• Move closer to the subject.
• Zoom in or use a longer focal length lens.

Keep It Simple

This next compositional tip is a logical extension of filling the frame. Almost all keen, novice photographers are guilty of trying capture too much – whether it's a landscape, portrait, architecture or still-life picture. It's difficult to know quite why this is – perhaps we're trying to provide the viewer with a more 'complete picture' of the scene in the hope that this will convey more powerfully what we want the viewer to see? But things work in exactly the opposite way – the less visually cluttered an image, the more powerful it becomes.

Pick your subject

One way of keeping your images simple is to pick a specific subject from the scene you're photographing. Say, for example, you're enjoying a holiday in a stunning tropical location and want to capture the sun, sea and sand. If you simply stand up and point your camera along the length of the beach and take a shot that includes just about everything you can see, you're likely to capture all the other sunbathers and swimmers, people walking down the beach, hotels and bars in the distance, and so on. When you show the image to friends and family back home,

ABOVE In this image, the tree, the moon and the foreground form three simple yet discrete elements, with the uniform blue sky adding to the image's simplicity.

they'll have a good idea of your physical environment, but not why your holiday was so special. However, pick a specific viewpoint, such as a trail of footprints in the wet sand or a colourful towel and beach umbrella and your shots will evoke a much greater response and the images will have a much greater visual impact.

BELOW These two images, which were taken at the same location, show the significant advantage of keeping your images simple. The photographer aimed to highlight the colourful house fronts juxtaposed against the yachts and dinghies. In the first image on the left, there is too much going on in the picture and no easily identifiable subject. By moving farther along the harbour wall, the photographer found a better position that not only provided an excellent view across to the houses, but also still captured the contrasting spirit of modernity in the modern sailing dinghies.

ABOVE A photograph of this parasol in its entirety would have meant including people and more of the building in the shot, which would reduce its impact.

ABOVE RIGHT The three main elements of this image, the window, door and drainpipe, provide a simple arrangement to the brick backdrop.

BELOW These simple footsteps in the sand are emotive, while also creating a graphic image. The surf and its recession have sorted the sand grains into clear patterns.

RIGHT We don't need to see the whole of this building to know that it was taken in an exotic location – the blue sky, terracotta walls, vibrant flowers and pristine white shutters suffice.

BELOW RIGHT A solitary figure placed in an urban setting can often create a powerful composition.

Rule of Thirds

One of the most popular and widely used compositional tools is the rule of thirds. The 'rule' was developed in the mid-19th century, primarily as a guide for landscape artists, but was quickly adopted by photographers who spotted its value, first in landscape photography, then in other genres.

Grid

When employing the rule of thirds the photographer mentally imposes a grid over a potential scene. The grid is comprised of two vertical and two horizontal lines that divide the scene into thirds, both vertically and horizontally, or into nine squares (see example on the right). The rule works on the basis that any continuous horizontal line running the width of the image, such as the horizon or a row of distant trees, has greater dynamism and interest if placed on one of the horizontal grid lines than if it were placed in the centre of the image. Similarly, any strong vertical objects in the scene would be best placed on one of the two vertical lines.

Points of interest

In addition to using horizontal and vertical lines as guides, it is also important to consider the four points at which the dividing lines cross – these are known as the points of interest or the points of power. When composing a shot, try to ensure that principal elements in the scene are placed over one or more of these points of interest. Doing so will ensure that focal points in your image are kept away from the centre of the picture and add interest to the image. You don't have to slavishly ensure that key objects sit directly over points of interest – they are intended as guidelines only.

LEFT The idea behind the rule of thirds is that it prevents you from placing the subject of a picture right in the middle of the frame, where there's a danger it will draw in viewers, and stop them from visually exploring the rest of the image. The image is divided into nine equal rectangles. Where the horizontal and vertical lines cross (the points of interest) is roughly where important elements of an image should be placed. This image is further balanced by the placement of the boat in the distance.

Portraits

Although the rule of thirds was devised primarily for landscape artists and photographers, it can also be used with other forms of photography. In portrait photography, for example, it is best to avoid having the subject's eyes run through the centre of the photograph if shooting a close-up of someone's head and shoulders. Instead place them along the top horizontal line. Similarly, if the portrait is a full-length shot, don't place the subject in the centre of the frame. Instead, try placing him or her along one of the two vertical lines.

In fact, the rule of thirds can apply to all styles or genres of photography – architecture and still life, as well as landscape and portraiture. It is worth bearing in mind, as mentioned earlier, rules are there to be learned, practised

RIGHT Portraits will often benefit if the subject's eyes are placed in line with the top horizontal rule.

Grid guidelines

The rule of thirds is a simple yet effective way of focusing the viewer's attention. Remember to:
- Mentally put horizontal or vertical lines in your image on thirds lines.
- Place key elements in your image on the four points of interest.

LEFT Like all composition 'rules', the rule of thirds is only a guide; there will be many times when placing the subject in the centre of the frame just feels right.

Viewfinder grid

On many of today's digital cameras, it is possible to electronically 'super-impose' a rule of thirds grid onto the viewfinder as you compose your image. As well as helping you to place the important elements of the scene on a point of interest, it can also help to remind you to hold the camera straight, so horizons or buildings don't slope off to one side.

and then broken. Once you try the rule of thirds for yourself, you'll likely find that many of your images become more balanced and dynamic. However, there are bound to be times when a piece of architecture or a tree just feels right when placed centrally, or when equal weight should be given to the land and the sky. In those instances, you should follow your gut instinct.

RIGHT In this silhouette shot of a boy throwing a stone, the figure has been deliberately placed in the right third of the shot. The composition is stronger and the stone consequently has 'space' into which it can be thrown.

BELOW Interestingly, research seems to show that compositions with one principal focal point are more successful if that element is positioned on the right-hand point of interest, rather than on the left, as we tend to look at images from left to right. It's thought that when the element is on the left, the viewer's eye stops travelling through the image as soon as it encounters its point of interest.

Frame within a Frame

Like the rule of thirds, a 'frame within a frame' is a technique first used by landscape artists and subsequently by photographers. There is a number of ways the technique can be used to create very different results.

Landscape

One of the most popular frame-within-a-frame techniques is used in landscape photography, where trees or other foreground subjects are used to frame a distant view. Although the technique has been widely used (to the point where many consider it somewhat hackneyed), it can still be very effective and usually helps add depth to the composition, as well as enhancing the significance of the

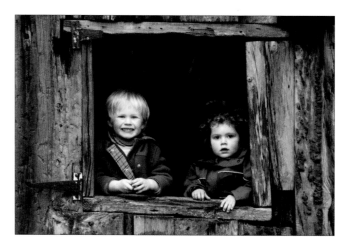

LEFT Frames not only help to focus the viewer's attention on the subject, they can also help photographers to pose their subjects for natural looking images.

▼ **BELOW** Using the branches of a tree is a classic way of framing a landscape image or a view of a historic building. Use this technique sparingly – it has been widely applied and is somewhat clichéd.

▼ **BELOW RIGHT** A more creative interpretation of the 'frame-within-a-frame' concept.

subject of the image. Also, the person viewing the image will often get a sense of the photographer's point of view, helping to create a shared experience of the scene and making the viewing all the more intimate.

Focus

To create the perception of depth, this technique usually works best if both the foreground 'border' and subject are in sharp focus, but it does pay to experiment. Walk farther back from the elements that you're intending to use as the border, use

your camera's zoom to close in on the distant subject and ensure that the camera doesn't focus on any of the foreground elements. If necessary, temporarily recompose the shot so that the foreground is out of the picture, then recompose the scene so that the foreground elements are once again in the frame, only now they should be out of focus. Take the picture and compare the effect of having a foreground that is either in or out of focus. Some photographs work far better with one technique than the other.

Portraits

This technique works in a slightly different way in portrait photography, as the subject is often within the object that is acting as the frame. Since the frame and subject are the same distance from the camera, you won't get the same perception of depth. Instead, the frame acts like a border, visually containing the subject and enhancing his or her significance. At the same time it will also contextualize the shot by putting the subject in a specific place or situation.

ABOVE When using a frame within your frame, experiment with the point of focus. Here, the doorway that acts as a frame is sharp, but the children in the background are out of focus.

TOP This image is about using frames within frames, although it has been taken further with the columns in the foreground and the smaller arched openings acting as frames.

ABOVE Sometimes the frames themselves can become the subject of the image. Here, the geometrical shape of the frame acts as the subject, making the viewer peer through to see the street.

RIGHT In this image the low-growing olive trees provide a frame or border for the bottom of the picture, while the bay is further framed by the rocky promontory near the top of the shot.

Point of View

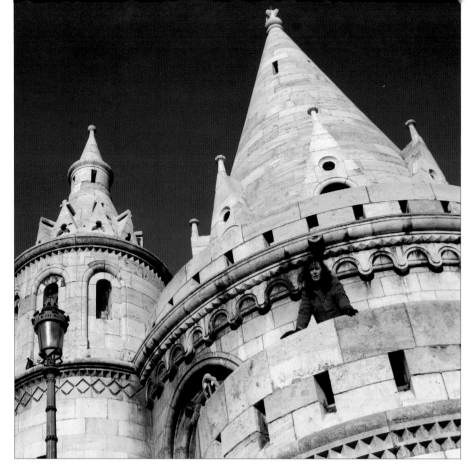

When looking through a series of images, one of the biggest clues that gives away the novice photographer is that all the images have been taken from a standing eye-level view. There's absolutely nothing wrong with this point of view – some of the most striking images have been shot from it – but by altering the camera height and angle every so often, you're not only more likely to create images with a fresh and exciting perspective, you'll also train your mind's eye to visualize scenes differently.

People

Of all the different genres, it is with portrait photography that changing your point of view (POV) can have the most dramatic impact. This is most likely down to the psychological responses we experience when communicating with other people. Generally we become aware in a very short space of time if we converse with someone at a radically different eye level. Somehow it just feels uncomfortable – reinforced by the expressions 'looking down on' or 'looking up to' someone. It's quite possible to recreate similar tensions by photographing people from above or below. However, be wary of overusing the technique. Just as we feel most comfortable talking to someone at the same level, so too do we feel most comfortable viewing portraits that have been taken at the same eye level. This is often most important when photographing

▲ **ABOVE** The low viewpoint allowed the photographer to get the top of the turrets in the shot, and it has also emphasized the angles of the building for added drama. If the photograph had been taken standing on the same level as the subject herself, it would have lost the sense of scale.

children and with close-up, head-and-shoulder portraits – it definitely pays to kneel down so that the camera is at the child's eye level.

▲ **ABOVE** When photographing a person sitting down, or a child, avoid pointing the camera down at the subject as this can create tension as he or she looks up into the camera.

▲ **ABOVE** By getting down to the same level as the subject, they can look directly into the camera, so avoiding any tension in their face from looking up or down at the camera.

▲ **ABOVE** Similarly, avoid photographing people from below unless you're trying to make them appear more powerful and authoritative or you are making a deliberate photographic point.

Camera angle

Just as shooting the same scene from different heights can provide new perspectives so, too, can trying out alternative angles. Generally we react most positively to accurately aligned horizons, but occasionally, with an appropriate subject matter, a skewed horizon or misaligned vertical can create a sense of unease and add drama to an image. Experiment with all sorts of varying angles to see what results you can achieve.

General photography

If you come across an interesting scene worthy of photographing, try experimenting with shots from different heights. Kneeling or lying down will provide new perspectives, as will finding something to stand on or finding a much higher viewpoint from which to shoot.

In addition, there's no rule that states that the camera must be held either vertically or horizontally straight. Try taking a few shots with the camera at an angle as this, too, may add a fresh perspective on a common scene. Any unusual viewpoint is likely to create an image that will attract and hold the viewer's attention.

ABOVE Shooting from a great height can sometimes provide a new perspective on a familiar scene, with shape, form and line being made more apparent.

RIGHT The unusual viewpoint of a copy of Michelangelo's David, which stands outside the Palazzo Vecchio in Florence, helps to maintain our attention.

BELOW Taken from eye level, these mushrooms would have become lost against the field. By getting down low and using a wide aperture to give a shallow depth of field, they've become the focus of this photograph and have been put in the context of their surroundings.

BELOW Photographing buildings, and specifically skyscrapers, from below helps to reinforce their size.

Shape and Form

The visual building blocks that make up our images can be thought of as shape and form. Often it is their proportion and relationship to the space they sit in that make the difference between a good image and a great one. For many photographers – and, in particular, those who have had little art education – it can sometimes be difficult to differentiate between shape and form. So, let's look in more detail at these two elements and see how they fit into the overall composition of an image.

Shape

The simplest way to visualize the difference between shape and form is to think of shape as two dimensional and form as three dimensional. Our concept of shape develops at a very early age, and is something that we encourage our children to learn. Our almost instantaneous and positive reaction to shapes can be successfully

exploited in photography, so try to make a habit of looking out for both natural and man-made objects that have clearly defined shapes. Start by looking out for simple outlines such as circles, squares and triangles and progress to shooting more complex shapes, such as flowers, architectural details, the crook of an elbow or the curve of a back.

Silhouette

As another type of shape, silhouettes are an effective way of exploiting the outlines and shapes made by specific objects, especially if photographed against a strong light, such as the sun or a full moon. Alternatively, for a portrait photograph, place a table

◀ **LEFT** Although the lighting is soft in this eye-catching photograph of decaying gears, the shadows between the teeth give them a three-dimensional form.

▲ **ABOVE** Light coming from the side casts shadows that are the best tool for helping to describe a subject's form.

light behind the person's head and ask him or her to turn their head 90° to the camera for the shot.

Form

Although silhouettes exploit our recognition and understanding of shape, they can appear very two-dimensional and lack 'body'. This is where form comes into play. To appreciate the three-dimensional aspect of an object, we need to see its form, and for us to fully appreciate the form, we need light and shade. Look for smooth, rounded objects and photograph them in soft, even lighting. The relationship between the light and dark areas provides us with the visual information we need to recognize the object's form.

▲ **ABOVE** In black and white photography, the relationship between the tones in an image is essential in describing the subject – without colour, it is only the interplay of light and dark that tells viewers what they are looking at.

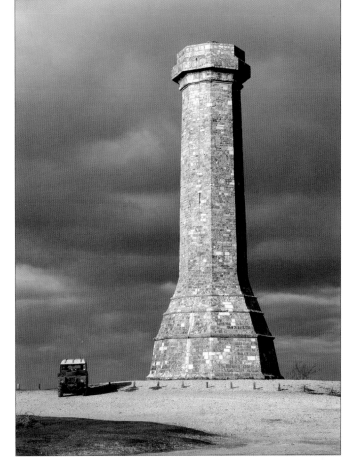

▲ **TOP** It's not always necessary to see every last detail to recognize what something is or evoke a response. Here we can almost feel the heat from the sun, while the silhouetted flag and chair suggest a beach setting.

▲ **ABOVE** Even objects as simple as the stone steps and iron railings to the entrance of this building can provide pleasing shape and form, here reinforced by the shadows thrown on to the steps.

▲ **ABOVE** Contrast plays a key part in describing form in a subject. Here, there is contrast between the lit and shaded sides of the monument, as well as between the light stone and brooding sky.

Pattern and Texture

Two other compositional tools to consider in photography are pattern and texture. Of the two, pattern is probably the visual element that you're less likely to think of as a strong compositional tool. When we think of patterns, many of us might initially consider the repetitive shapes and colours found in wallpaper or curtains, whose function is sometimes to create a visually relaxing backdrop that doesn't overly stimulate our senses or attract attention.

Lateral thinking

So how can you use a pattern to provide a visually stimulating image? As a photographer, your aim should be to provide a view of the world that others have not considered before. Spotting patterns in everyday objects and scenes will provide a fresh and new perspective on the world. More

▼ **BELOW** Interesting patterns are all around us – we just don't tend to notice them. If you look a little harder, you will find potential subjects everywhere, such as these neatly aligned mobile homes.

obvious examples include a row of flowers of a similar shape, the uniform ripples in an area of sand, a tiled floor, a brick wall or a flight of stairs. But what about a row of identical cars on a production line or hundreds of stacked cargo containers? These all have the repetitive elements of pattern, and if shot sensitively – in the right light and following some of the other rules of composition discussed already – they

▲ **ABOVE** There's a good contrast in this image between the regular pattern of the windows themselves and the irregularity of the old buildings reflected in the glass.

can create a striking image and, depending on the subject matter, may also convey a message.

Remember to look out for elements that break the pattern, as this will help to create an even stronger composition. Supposing in the sea of red cars or containers one or two were blue or silver – both would break the pattern and add drama. Once you've spotted a pattern, don't simply record it and move on. Consider other angles that might reveal other patterns that you had not seen initially.

Proximity and light

Unlike pattern, texture seems to have a much more immediate relevance and resonance as a compositional tool. Our sense of touch is highly developed and at times seems to have a direct link to our sense of sight – we only have to look at an object and in most cases we know instantly how it will feel to touch it. Teasing out the texture in the objects we photograph will, therefore, elicit a strong response from viewers, even though they know it is simply a two-dimensional image of the object.

To really appreciate the texture of individual objects, you'll often need to focus as close as you can to the object you're photographing. Light needs to meet the object's surface at 45° or less so that the object casts shadows, which emphasize the texture itself. To ensure the texture is as pronounced as possible, the object is best lit from one side, as this will create the strongest shadows. So, if you're shooting outdoors and you want to capture the texture of peeling paint on an old wall (at 90° vertical), shoot when the sun is high in the sky (at around midday). However, if the object is flat on the ground, shoot early in the morning or late in the afternoon when the sun is lower.

Although we usually get in close to isolate an object's texture, this isn't a hard and fast rule. Texture can also be appreciated on a much larger scale, particularly if it helps to convey an emotion or message. For a texture-filled landscape, for example, set your lens to its widest angle and get low down to the ground to ensure you focus as close as you can to what's beneath you. Point the camera up slightly so that the distant view is also visible and then make a couple of exposures.

Composing with Lines: Horizontals

In photographic composition, lines, no matter how they are formed, whether artificial or natural, are a key element – from the horizontal horizon of a serene landscape, through the powerful, towering verticals of a cityscape, to the diagonal lines that can lead a viewer's eye through a photograph.

On the next few pages, we will look at how lines can add structure to a composition, and how – if badly managed – they can spoil an otherwise good composition.

Landscapes

Horizontal lines in the composition of an image are likely to be most apparent in landscape photography, where a horizontal format best suits the subject matter. Horizontal lines tend to imbue an image with a feeling of calm and stability, and even timelessness and permanency.

BELOW The unbroken horizon works well with the much smaller broken horizontals of these hay bales.

Horizons

The most commonly occurring horizontal line is the horizon of a landscape or seascape, which will often be the basis from which the rest of the image emanates. An unbroken horizon can sometimes make an image appear flat and lifeless, so try to punctuate it with other elements, such as trees, hills or buildings, unless

ABOVE This image mixes horizontals and verticals. The groynes, clouds and the sea form strong horizontals, but the groynes themselves are also vertical, contrasting with the clouds.

BELOW The repetitive horizontal lines of the bridges running off into the distance create a sense of tranquillity in this late afternoon photograph of Prague.

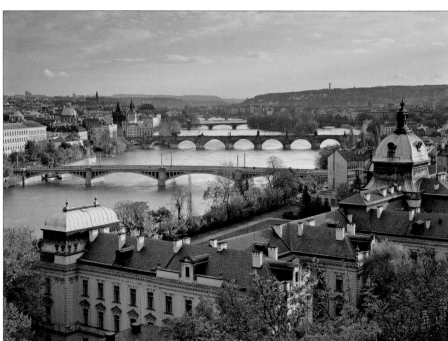

you're trying to convey a specific message or visual impact. Additionally, concentrate on ensuring that the horizon is as straight as possible.

Rule of thirds

When deciding where the horizon should be positioned in your image, remember the rule of thirds (see pages 50–51). As a general rule, images tend to work better if the horizon is either a third up or down the image – but this is only a guideline and there are plenty of successful images that feature horizons in the centre of the frame. Horizontals also help to add depth to photographs by providing visual breaks. Think of a view down a city river that features a number of bridges or a landscape image that shows fields of different crops running off into the distance.

Portrait format

If there are a number of strong horizontals in the scene, try turning your camera through 90° and taking a portrait-format photograph. Too many horizontals can cause the eye to tire, but as a portrait-format shot, the eye will tend to look down and register the depth of the image.

◄ **ABOVE RIGHT** When an image displays so many horizontals that the image, if shot in landscape format, would tire the eye. In these instances, it's better to shoot portrait.

► **RIGHT** The numerous broken horizontals of the roofs of the houses add to the chaotic atmosphere of this image.

Straight horizontals

If horizontals are a significant element of an image's composition, it's essential that they are straight. If you don't intend to edit your images on computer, use a tripod with built-in levels to ensure horizontals are exactly straight.

Composing with Lines: Verticals

Like horizontals, vertical lines can also convey strong emotions. Power, grandeur and strength are all words that are associated with images that feature numerous vertical lines.

Many of the rules that apply to horizontals also apply to verticals, not least trying to keep them parallel to the edge of the image. This can be quite difficult, as they often feature in images in which the camera has been pointed upward in order to capture the entire scene. This can create the problem of 'converging verticals', where a building or other tall object seems to grow increasingly narrow the higher up you look. It's the same as the vanishing point effect in which railway lines appear to reach a single point as they stretch out into the distance – only with converging verticals you're looking 'up' rather than 'along'.

If you have a single, vertical object in the image, use the rule of thirds and don't place it in the middle of the frame, unless the resulting symmetry adds to the composition.

Landscape format

Most photographs that contain strong verticals are usually shot with the camera held vertically, not only to better accommodate the image, but also to accentuate the height of the vertical lines. As with horizontals, however, it doesn't always have to be this way. Experiment by shooting the odd frame in landscape format. Numerous vertical lines all in a row can accentuate the width of the scene or form a pattern. In addition, try to remember that your images will be reproduced in two dimensions and visualize this when you are out taking photographs. For example, lines that are painted on a flat road

▶ **RIGHT** The strong vertical lines of the trees are exaggerated and emphasized by choosing a portrait-format shape for this photograph.

▼ **BELOW** The verticality of many modern cities makes for very dramatic images and conveys a sense of scale.

leading off into the distance will translate as converging verticals in your two-dimensional image, adding not only a sense of depth to the image but also leading the eye.

▶ **RIGHT** Look out for the pattern that occurs in repeating vertical structures.

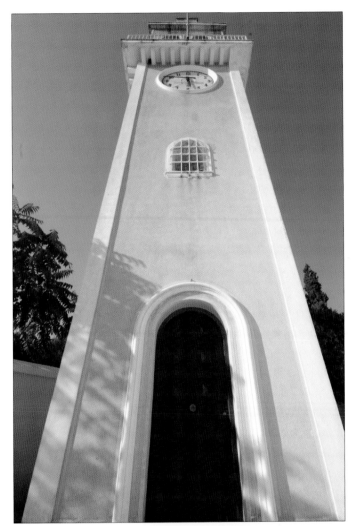

▲ **ABOVE** The height of this imposing bell tower has been exaggerated by using a wide-angle lens placed at the base of the tower and pointed upward.

▶ **RIGHT** The mix of vertical lines in the field and the horizontal row of trees in the distance work in either a portrait or landscape format, with the horizon remaining central in the frame.

Composing with Lines: Diagonals

While strong vertical and horizontal lines provide structure to an image and create visual boundaries, they can at times 'ground' an image, making it solid yet static. If you want to add a sense of movement to an image, look for strong diagonal lines instead. These tend to produce the most dynamic results and lead the viewer's eye through an image, especially when they lead to the subject of the photograph.

Symmetry

It's unlikely that it would happen, but avoid recording a line that runs directly from one corner of the image to another. Diagonals work better when they appear from one-third/two-thirds up or one-third/two-thirds along the frame – and usually from bottom left if they are to serve as a leading line.

Of course, if you're trying to show how different two areas of a specific scene are, then dividing them exactly in half with a diagonal that runs corner to corner may well provide a striking image.

▲ **ABOVE** The diagonal representation of this common wildlife scene helps to make the image a little more dynamic.

▼ **BELOW** The breaking waves form a diagonal, leading the viewer to San Francisco's famous Golden Gate Bridge – the subject of the image.

▲ **ABOVE** Diagonal lines work best when they don't run from corner to corner, but instead enter the frame one-third or two-thirds up or across the image, as in this shot of a lone ski lift chair.

Most of the time, one diagonal line will be enough to add dynamic effect and to lead the viewer's eye into the frame, but look out also for clashing diagonals as these can add tension to an image and create a sense of chaos (which may or may not be a good thing).

Vanishing point

One of the most powerful ways in which diagonals are used is when they converge to create a vanishing point. When we first think of vanishing points, we usually think of the somewhat clichéd railway tracks or roads, but vanishing points occur naturally as well, it's just that they're usually less well-defined in form, tone or colour. For example, you may find you can create a vanishing point by using a diagonal line of clouds converging on a hedge that runs from you into the distance.

ABOVE The wall in this image runs diagonally, but it isn't that successful as it runs across the frame in the wrong direction – from left to right and out of the frame.

BELOW The raking diagonal highlights add to the sense of movement and purpose in this shot, and create a contrast with the pattern of the tiled floor.

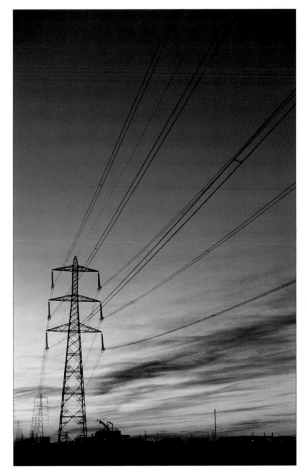

ABOVE The converging diagonals of the power lines take the viewer into the shot and out the other side.

Composing with Curves

Lines – whether horizontal, vertical or diagonal – can all help to add structure, inject movement and elicit specific emotional responses from a composition. But what do curves do for an image? Curves, like diagonals, tend to add dynamism and movement to an image and help to lead the viewer's eye through it. Furthermore, several conflicting curves can add tension and chaos to a composition.

S-curve

The most powerful compositional curve is the S-shaped curve, or S-curve. This not only provides motion to an image, but it also adds balance and grace. Look out for S-curves both in nature, such as a meandering river or the edge of a stand of trees, or ones that have been made artificially, such as a winding path. The latter provide a visual way through the image and suggest to the viewer both a literal and metaphorical journey.

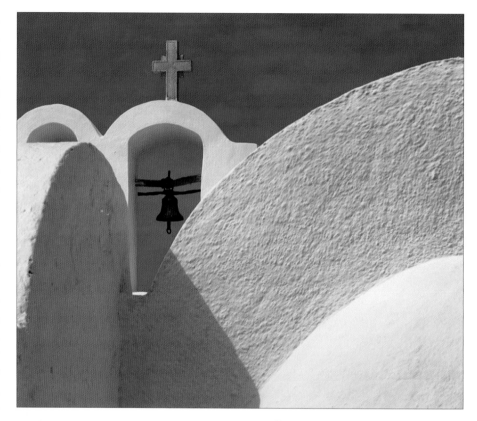

ABOVE The curves of this Greek Orthodox church contrast against the vertical and horizontal lines of the cross.

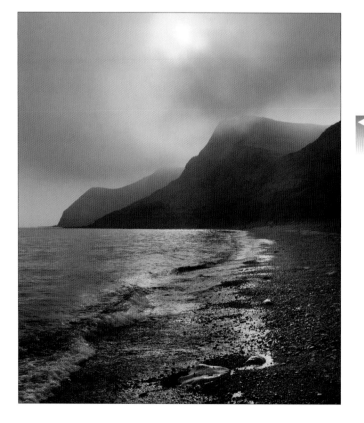

LEFT Most of the compositional curves that appear in photographs are likely to be made up of something solid and fairly permanent – such as hedgerows, roads or river courses – but remember you're freezing an instant in time, during which anything can form a curve for a short time.

Leading lines

During our discussion of diagonal lines and curves, there has been a number of references to 'leading lines' and 'leading the eye'. As their names suggest, leading lines lead the viewer into the image, and should ideally lead the viewer's gaze to the subject of the image.

Leading lines tend to work best when they start from the bottom left of the frame, as it's more natural for the eye to 'read' from left to right. An important tip to consider, however, is that while it's good practice and recommended that the line can lead in from an edge, in most cases it's unwise to have it running out of the frame at the other side. The reasoning behind this is that while you want to encourage viewers into the frame with a leading line, you don't want them then to follow the line out of the frame, without stopping and considering the image for a while.

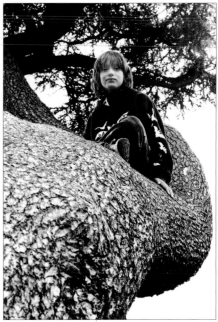

BELOW In this image, the curve of the tree wraps around the figure, drawing our attention to the subject.

BELOW The slight S-shape to the remains of the sea at low tide adds movement to this image, as well as drawing our attention to the boat.

Using curves

When walking around looking for potential landscape images, remember that not all landscapes are shot with a wide-angle lens or zoom setting. Telephoto lenses or settings can reveal compositional elements that were not immediately visible with wide-angle lenses.

TOP Curves, like diagonals, can act as leading lines, taking or guiding the viewer through an image. The most successful are leading lines or curves that lead the viewer from the edge of the frame into the body of the image where the subject can be found.

ABOVE Here, a rusty old mooring chain revealed only at low tide acts as a leading line curve to the house beyond.

Landscape versus Portrait

A clue to the novice photographer's picture collection is that it's likely to contain images shot solely in the horizontal, landscape shape, or format. Convention used to dictate that landscapes were shot horizontally and portraits vertically, but it doesn't have to be that way, and nor should it be.

Fresh perspective

There are plenty of examples when turning the camera through 90° will provide you with a much better shape for your landscape image. Trees obviously spring to mind, especially if you've had to retire some distance to fit your subject into the landscape format. By photographing a golden, autumnal tree in the vertical format, not only are you more likely to be able to get closer, you'll also avoid having unwanted elements to the left and right of the tree in the frame.

ABOVE Not all portraits have to be taken in an upright, portrait format – the rules can be broken. The lines of the gate and the gatepost contain this image, while the subject is perfectly placed using the rule of thirds.

There are many examples where shooting landscapes vertically will offer a much more complementary framing shape – mountains, valleys and rivers may all benefit from this treatment. Try to get into the habit of framing a potential landscape in the vertical format, even if you've successfully captured the scene in the more conventional horizontal landscape format. After a while, you'll look at landscapes in different ways and when you come to show your images to other people, particularly when putting a small portfolio or exhibition together, you'll be grateful for the variety of images in both shapes.

LEFT Using a portrait format has emphasized the shape of the terracing of these paddy fields and helped to add depth to the fields in the distance.

Architecture

Buildings and cityscapes offer more opportunities to experiment with both horizontal- and vertical-format photographs. Once you've become used to turning your camera, you'll start to see how certain elements make for an attractive landscape format image, while changing your angle or point of view slightly may bring other background elements into play that would make for a more pleasing portrait-format shot.

In context

While full-length portraits lend themselves to the vertical format, not all portraits need to be shot this way. A landscape format may be the better option, depending on the position of your subject's arms – especially if outstretched – or whether you want to include contextualizing background. Also, don't forget the rule of thirds. Even if the portrait is just a head-and-shoulders shot, you may want to position the subject to one side to avoid it being in the centre of the frame.

LEFT AND BELOW Both of these images are of the same scene taken from an identical viewpoint, but they both look very different. In the first image (left), a wide-angle lens and portrait format show us much more of the scene, while in the second image (below), a long focal length lens and a landscape format create a tightly cropped picture.

LEFT It pays to experiment with a landscape or portrait format. Here the photographer has used a portrait format to emphasize the long reflection of the sun on the sea.

ABOVE In this landscape version, the sun's reflection plays a less important role, but the wider format includes more of the delicately coloured sky and the calming horizontal of the land.

Compositional Balance

When you look at certain images, particularly those that feature two or more key elements, you may often get a sense that things aren't quite right, although the reason for this is not immediately apparent. If so, it may be that the image is unbalanced in terms of its composition.

Vertical axis

Balance in composition is mostly determined by how well the primary elements of the image are divided by the vertical axis that runs more or less down the centre of the image.

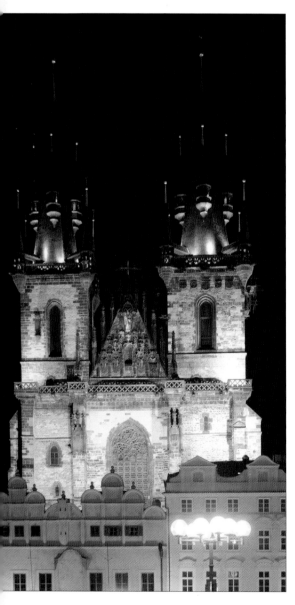

Balance can also be achieved through the horizontal axis, such as the reflection of a tree in a pond.

Symmetrical balance

The easiest and most straightforward compositional balance is often referred to as 'symmetrical' balance. As its name suggests, symmetrical balance is achieved when two objects of equal 'weight' are positioned on either side of the central vertical dividing line, so that one object on one side of the image balances out the other object on the other side.

Symmetrical balance creates a sense of stability, order and tranquillity in an image, and it is used successfully in architectural photography, formal group portraits and for any number of 'artificial' landscapes, such as an avenue of trees or a formal garden.

Asymmetrical balance

While symmetrical compositions certainly provide visual balance and bring a sense of order and calm to an image, viewing a succession of symmetrically balanced images would ultimately be a rather dull and boring affair. Of much greater visual interest are asymmetrically balanced images. These can provide a sense of depth to an image and are much more dynamic, but you do need to think harder about how balance is achieved.

Asymmetrical balance works on the basis that objects in an image each have their own visual 'mass' – whether it's their physical size, how colourful they are, how bright they are, whether or not the object is in focus and so on. A well-balanced image will have the various components arranged in such a way

◀ **LEFT** This picture is a strong example of a symmetrically balanced composition, where the two towers in the background balance each other perfectly.

▲ **ABOVE** This scene also relies heavily on a symmetrical composition to balance the image – in this case with the row of trees and their reflections in the water.

that their various 'weights' are balanced. For example, objects with greater contrast have more weight than low-contrasting elements, therefore to achieve balance the low-contrasting element needs to be bigger than the high-contrasting one.

There's no quick way to master asymmetrical balance, and rather than stifling your creativity by

▲ **ABOVE** Colourful subjects and larger subjects may carry more weight in a composition, but this is balanced here by the figure in the foreground being in sharp focus.

rigidly sticking to the 'rules', it's better to keep shooting and simply be aware of how objects of a different size, colour, contrast and visual appeal interact with each other.

▲ **ABOVE** This asymmetrical composition is well balanced thanks to the colours of the sea and the sand, their relative sizes and the isolated subjects at the bottom and top.

Asymmetry in action

It is important to be aware of the weight that the different components in an image carry. The basic ideas are:

- An object at the edge of the frame has more weight than a centred one.
- Irregular shapes have more weight than regular ones.
- Colourful elements carry more weight than less-colourful ones.
- Isolated objects carry more weight than those that are surrounded by other objects.
- More interesting objects attract greater attention than less interesting ones. For example, people's faces have greater weight than buildings or landmarks.
- Objects in focus take precedence over out-of-focus objects.
- Objects being looked at by people in an image gain emphasis.

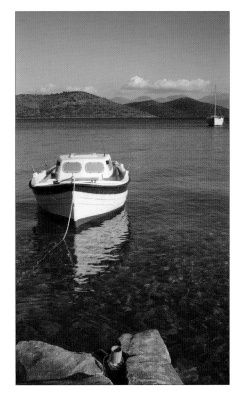

▲ **ABOVE** While our attention is initially grabbed by the larger boat in the foreground, the image is balanced thanks to the smaller boat in the background and to the right.

▲ **ABOVE** Symmetrical balance is easily achieved in this image of an avenue of trees in a misty parkland setting. The trees also create a pleasing vanishing point.

Basic Composition – Try It Yourself

Now that we've looked at some of the basic compositional tips, it's time to get shooting. Below is a short summary of the compositional 'rules' discussed so far, with some key assignments that will help you to explore them further so you can begin to see for yourself how following some of the rules some of the time can help make your images more dynamic. Remember, it's important not to get too tied up with these rules, particularly if you start to find that you're not taking any photos at all because your scenes don't apparently meet any of the compositional requirements. Often a scene will look inviting, yet you can't quite understand why. Don't stop and try to work out what compositional rules it's fulfilling; simply take the shot and review your image later.

Keep it simple

Take several shots that make it very clear to the viewer what the subject of the picture is. Try to ensure there isn't any marginal clutter or any other distracting objects.

Framing

Shape and form

Fill the frame

Fill the frame

Take a few shots of different objects that appeal to you because of their shape, colour or form, or because the light reflecting off them is attractive. Really zoom into the subject to ensure that there is no surrounding clutter.

Rule of thirds

Try to find different scenes that fulfil the 'rule of thirds'. Bear in mind that you don't have to find four key elements to fit all the 'points of interest'. Sometimes just one or two will do to make an effective composition.

Framing

Create some instances where you have the opportunity of putting a frame within a frame. Remember that the key word is 'create', so you can be proactive here and take a picture of someone looking through a window or even take a shot looking out of a window. Bear in mind that the frame should ideally be attractive in its own right and it should also complement the subject of the image in some way.

Camera height and camera angle

Take some shots with a radically altered camera height and others using different camera angles. The objective is to give a fresh perspective to a scene that will make the viewer take a closer look at the image.

Shape and form

Remember that we tend to use two-dimensional shape to recognize objects, while form gives an object a three-dimensional appearance. Take several shots of various objects so that the viewer gets only a sense of its shape, and then use different lighting conditions or a different angle to take some more shots of the same objects that provide the viewer with a sense of the objects' form.

Vertical lines

Landscape versus portrait

Leading lines

Pattern and texture

A fun and surprisingly rewarding exercise; simply take several images that exploit an object's pattern or texture. Remember to consider the angle of the light to emphasize texture, and think laterally about what constitutes 'pattern'.

Horizontals and verticals

Shoot a few objects or scenes that evoke a sense of peace and calm due to the presence of horizontal lines and three objects or scenes that use vertical lines.

Working with diagonals

Look out for scenes in which a diagonal line leads the viewer through the image. Ideally it should take the viewer to the subject of the photograph.

Curves and leading lines

S-curves and leading lines help viewers into the image, and ideally take them to the subject of the image. Look for S-curves and leading lines in both nature and man-made scenes and try to take five images that feature these compositional aids.

Portrait versus landscape

When you find a good subject for a photograph, it's worth considering the benefits of turning the camera through 90° to see if it provides a fresh perspective. Remember that landscapes don't always have to be shot in a landscape format, and nor do portraits always have to be shot in the standard portrait format.

Compositional balance

From now on, try to think about achieving compositional balance in your images. If one of the subjects of your image is large, try to offset it with one that is smaller, but pushed more to the edge of the image area, or is more colourful, brighter, has greater visual appeal and so on.

Texture

Creative Capture

Armed with a sound knowledge of the camera's settings, we put that knowledge to more creative uses in this chapter. The key principles of exposure, depth of field and selective focusing are covered – all of which are essential concepts to understand in order to advance your photography. Also explored is the significance of shutter speed and how it can be used to creative effect. We take a look at lighting and the pivotal role it plays when taking photographs. Finally, following a review of focal length, the chapter concludes with an examination of black and white photography and how to achieve stunning black and white photographs in the digital age.

Understanding Exposure

The most fundamental technical aspect of photography is perhaps exposure. The positive news for experienced film photographers is that when it comes to exposure, digital cameras behave almost exactly like film cameras. For those who are new to photography, exposure governs whether a picture is too bright, too dark or just right – although this is often subjective.

There are three settings that govern exposure – the shutter speed (which determines how long the sensor is exposed to light); the aperture (which determines how much light reaches the sensor); and the ISO setting (which determines the sensitivity of the sensor – see page 14). These three elements combine to provide a specific exposure – if one element is altered, one of the other two settings must also change if the same exposure is to be retained.

Shutter speed and aperture

To provide complete information about a specific exposure you need to know the shutter speed (usually a fraction of a second, but it can be much longer than a second), the aperture (expressed as an 'f'-number) and the ISO setting; this is why you will often see an exposure setting written as $^1/_{125}$ sec at f/5.6 (ISO 200). If these individual settings provided the 'correct' exposure, then altering one setting without altering either of the other two would result in an 'inaccurate' exposure. For example, if the shutter speed was reduced by half to $^1/_{250}$ sec, the image would be underexposed. If, however, at the same time the shutter speed was reduced by half the size of the aperture was doubled (from f/5.6 to f/4), or the ISO setting was increased to 400, then the exposure would remain the same – in this way, $^1/_{125}$ sec at

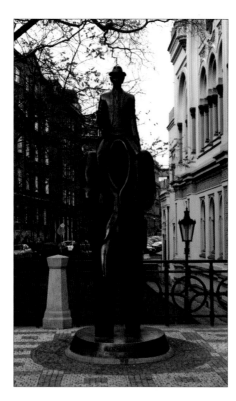

f/5.6 (ISO 200) provides the same exposure as $^1/_{250}$ sec at f/4 (ISO 200), which in turn provides the same exposure as $^1/_{250}$ sec at f/5.6 (ISO 400).

ISO settings

It is only since the advent of digital photography that the ISO setting has played such an integral part in governing exposure. Previously, the relationship between shutter speed and aperture primarily governed the exposure, since you couldn't change the film in a camera with every shot. Now that digital ISO can be altered at will, this setting can be used in a proactive way to get the optimum exposure for every shot you take. The lowest ISO setting will always provide the best image quality, so you should aim to use the lowest possible ISO setting at all times (especially if you're using a compact camera), and only increase the sensitivity if, for example, there's a risk of camera shake due to slow shutter speed.

ABOVE In difficult lighting situations such as this, where a dark subject appears in front of a light background, the camera may underexpose the subject (as seen on the left) if left on Auto. By manually enlarging the aperture, the subject is accurately exposed (on the right).

Low ISO

Assuming, that you set the ISO at the lowest possible setting (while still being able to hold the camera without the risk of camera shake), it's the relationship between shutter speed and aperture that will ultimately dictate the exposure.

As we shall see over the coming pages, these are the two most important elements to control. The aperture setting determines the depth of field (how much of the scene is sharply in focus) while shutter speed determines whether a moving object is blurred or not. Aside from general composition, these two photographic controls govern how your images will look.

ABOVE These three images were taken at the same time of day, but they appear very different. Using a tripod to ensure the scene was exactly the same, the first shot, the darkest, was given a manual exposure of f/5 at $^1/_{3200}$ sec (ISO 200); the second shot was taken using f/5 at $^1/_{200}$ sec (ISO 200); while the final image, the brightest image, was exposed at f/5 at $^1/_{16}$ sec (ISO 200). Manually altering the shutter speed has greatly affected the exposure of each shot.

| f/2 | f/2.8 | f/4 | f/5.6 | f/8 | f/11 | f/16 | f/22 |

EXPOSURE ALTERNATIVES

Aperture	f/2	f/2.8	f/4	f/5.6	f/8	f/11	f/16	f/22
Shutter speed	$^1/_{1000}$	$^1/_{500}$	$^1/_{250}$	$^1/_{125}$	$^1/_{60}$	$^1/_{30}$	$^1/_{15}$	$^1/_{8}$
ISO	100	100	100	100	100	100	100	100

LEFT This sequence of graphics shows the range of aperture sizes available on camera lenses. Not all lenses will have such a wide range; many for example will only offer from f/4 to f/16, but the diagram shows how the higher the number; the smaller the aperture. This has a direct bearing on depth of field. It also shows that changing the aperture from f/5.6 to f/8 halves the amount of light reaching the sensor, or alternatively how changing the aperture from f/16 to f/11 doubles the amount of light reaching the aperture.

ISO ALTERNATIVES (TABLE A)

Aperture	f/2.8	f/4	f/5.6	f/8	f/11	f/16
Shutter speed	$^1/_{30}$	$^1/_{30}$	$^1/_{30}$	$^1/_{30}$	$^1/_{30}$	$^1/_{30}$
ISO	100	200	400	800	1600	3200

ISO ALTERNATIVES (TABLE B)

Aperture	f/2.8	f/2.8	f/2.8	f/2.8	f/2.8	f/2.8
Shutter speed	$^1/_{30}$	$^1/_{60}$	$^1/_{250}$	$^1/_{500}$	$^1/_{1000}$	$^1/_{2000}$
ISO	100	200	400	800	1600	3200

LEFT With digital cameras, ISO setting plays a much more proactive role in determining exposure. If settings of f/2.8 at $^1/_{30}$ sec with ISO 100 provide an accurate exposure, by changing the ISO setting you will also either have to change the aperture (Table A) or the shutter speed (Table B). For example, in Table A changing the ISO to 800 has enabled an aperture of f/8 to be used, which provides much greater depth of field than f/2.8, so more of the image will be in focus. In Table B, changing the ISO to 800 has enabled a shutter speed of $^1/_{500}$ sec, which would be much more appropriate for fast-moving action.

Manual Exposure

Up to now, we've concentrated on the camera's various preset automatic and semi-automatic settings and modes found on almost all digital cameras. These help us to obtain sharply focused and accurately exposed photographs between 80–90% of the time in a variety of popular shooting scenarios. For many people, understanding these modes and settings will provide them with everything they need to get the photographs they want. However, if you want to stretch your creativity, take control and make the most of your camera in more challenging lighting conditions, it's important to understand how to use your camera in its Manual (M) mode. Experimenting with a variety of shutter and aperture settings with the camera in Manual, ensures that you end up with more accurately exposed images – more consistently.

Exposure

Having discussed how the relationship between aperture and shutter speed (and ISO setting) works to determine exposure, we're halfway there to understanding how to use a camera in its Manual mode.

With the camera in Manual you set both the shutter speed and the aperture independently of one another. This can lead to horrendous exposure miscalculations, particularly if you're used to using automatic or semi-automatic modes. You may, for example, set the shutter speed to $^1/_{500}$ of a second (sec) to freeze action and an aperture setting of f/11 to get as much of the scene as possible in focus, but unless you're in anything other than an extremely bright lighting situation at the time you press the shutter release, you're going to end up with a very underexposed image.

Alternatively, in the heat of the action, you may simply forget that the aperture is set on f/4 and keep firing away only to find that all your images are overexposed.

Viewfinder scale bar

To help you obtain the correct exposure in Manual mode, look through the viewfinder and there should be a form of scale bar. It will usually have a '0' in the centre and then some marks to both left and right (or above and below), with perhaps the figures '-1' and '-2' to the left (or below) and '(+)1' and '(+)2' to the right (above). The '0' indicates 'correct' exposure, while the minus figures indicate slight underexposure and the positive figures overexposure. Each mark is referred to as a 'stop', so +2 indicates 2 stops overexposed. You'll notice that as you adjust either the aperture or shutter speed settings, the marker will indicate the new exposure on the scale bar.

Aim for 'zero'

While ideally you're trying to 'zero' the exposure, anything within the -2 to +2 range will usually provide a usable image. In fact, this is the whole point of shooting in Manual mode. You may in fact find that when you review your images, the one with a -1 or even -2 setting (slightly underexposed) provides a better overall image than '0', which is theoretically more accurately exposed. This is down to complex lighting situations when the camera's metering system, however sophisticated, is not able to read your mind and know exactly what it is you're exposing for. For example, with the camera set in an automatic mode, in very shadowy conditions, the camera will often

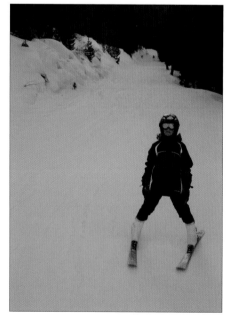

LEFT AND ABOVE Under certain lighting conditions, especially those in which there is a lot of reflected light, the camera's metering system is likely to underexpose the scene (as on the right). In cases such as this, exposure will need to be set manually.

overexpose the subject as the dark ambient light tricks the metering system into thinking it's darker than it really is. Similarly, in very light conditions, such as snow scenes, the opposite will often occur – the bright, reflected light will fool the camera into thinking it's brighter than it really is and underexpose the subject. When ready to shoot, set an appropriate exposure (aiming for close to 'zero'), take a shot and review the results using the histogram and image preview on the LCD. Adjust any settings if necessary and fire the shutter again.

If at any point during your exposure adjustment the pointer reaches the end of the scale bar and flashes, this may well indicate that the image, if taken, will be so over- or under-exposed that it will be un-usable.

Creativity

One of the principal reasons for using Manual mode is when you deliberately want an under- or over-exposed image for creative reasons. In any automatic or semi-automatic setting the camera will always aim to achieve a 'correct' exposure. As we'll see later, shooting in Manual mode is also often the only way to capture very low-light or night scenes.

Doubtless you'll find that when you first start shooting in Manual mode you'll work more slowly and make a number of exposure errors, but stick with it and you'll soon be reaping the benefits.

▲ **ABOVE** Cameras with less sophisticated metering systems, such as centre-weighted metering, are more likely to get exposure wrong. Here the camera has exposed for the plants (left) resulting in an overexposed beach. Reducing the exposure by 2 stops (right) resulted in a far better photograph.

▶ **RIGHT** Many cameras have a 'blown highlight warning' facility. When switched on, any 'blown' highlights in an image, when reviewed on the LCD screen, will flash (here shown in red) to let you know parts of the image are entirely overexposed.

BRACKETING

Most advanced compacts and dSLR cameras have the ability to 'bracket' images. Usually described as 'auto exposure bracketing' (AEB), the camera will fire three shots in quick succession, each with a slightly different exposure compensation setting. The amount of compensation can be pre-selected, but usually it's $1/3$-stop, $1/2$-stop and 1-stop (i.e. the bracketed images would be say '$-1/3$, 0, $+1/3$' or '$-1/2$, 0, $+1/2$'. The images below were bracketed a full stop.

| Exposure -1 stop | Exposure 0 | Exposure +1 stop |

Manual Focus

With digital camera manufacturers spending so much money on research and development into increasingly sophisticated autofocus modes, a novice photographer might wonder why we need to focus manually?

While your camera's autofocusing system is likely to provide sharp images the majority of the time, as we've already seen, there are occasions when even the most advanced autofocus modes can fail to work. These include in low-light conditions when the camera cannot 'see' well enough, or when there is insufficient contrast for the camera to detect the point of focus. Similarly, if there are a number of potential subjects, the camera may not know which one to focus on. While you can often select a specific focus point that the camera will use as its reference point, it can sometimes be quicker to focus manually.

In addition, focusing manually may be necessary when the main subject of an image is behind a distracting foreground, such as a window, iron railings or the bars of a cage. In these instances, the camera's autofocusing system may continually try to focus

▲ **ABOVE** In landscape photography, there's little need for a fast autofocusing system. With subjects like this, the camera may not always focus where you want it to.

▼ **BELOW** This image was taken through an airplane window. The photographer manually focused on the land in case the camera autofocused on the window.

Focus ring

Cameras that are best suited for manual focus are those that feature a focus ring on the camera lens, such as dSLRs or fixed-lens dSLR-like cameras. Although many compacts have a manual focus option, this will often involve the use of buttons, which can be cumbersome to operate, slow to react and use up valuable power. A manual focus ring, on the other hand, is quick, intuitive and uses no power.

on the foreground object rather than the background – switch to manual and your problems are solved.

Shutter lag

In our earlier discussion of autofocus modes, we covered the issue of shutter lag, which is particularly apparent in sports and action photography. One way to avoid this annoying time lag is to set the focus to manual and prefocus on the area in which the action is about to take place. Half press the shutter release so that the camera makes its other calculations, such as setting the correct exposure and white balance, and as soon as the subject comes into view, fire the shutter. This can work using autofocus as long as the camera has something to focus on that is on the same focal plane as the action, but often the area you'll want to focus on is empty until filled by the action, and the camera may well focus on an object beyond the area of interest. Of course this will only work in those sports, such as motor racing, in which you can predict where the action is going to take place.

Close up/macro

In some instances, especially with close-up or macro photography, it becomes almost impossible to use autofocus, as the subject is so close to the lens. As we'll discover, more often than not, it's much easier to set the camera to manual focus and the lens to its shortest focusing distance, and physically move the camera backward and forward, until the specific element you're trying to capture is in focus.

ABOVE LEFT Using manual focus may well be the only way to deliberately shoot a scene out of focus for creative effect.

ABOVE With low light scenes, focusing manually is essential as very few cameras will be able to 'see' to focus in such dark lighting conditions.

BELOW LEFT An increasing number of dSLRs feature 'Live View', in which the LCD screen can be used to focus a shot. This is a more convenient way of focusing macro shots.

BELOW If your camera's autofocus can't keep up with fast-moving subjects, pre-focus on the ground, for example, on which the action will take place and wait for your subject to enter the frame.

Depth of Field

Focus on farthest trees

Although we've yet to cover the topic in detail, the term 'depth of field' has already cropped up in numerous places. That's unavoidable as, after 'exposure', it is the second most fundamental aspect of photography.

Depth of field (DoF) is a technical way of describing how much of an image is in focus – its 'zone of sharpness'. An image with narrow or short depth of field is one that has a small zone of sharpness, while an image with a wide depth of field has a large zone of sharpness.

Point and shoot

If, up until now, you've been using a point-and-shoot camera, you may never have given depth of field a second thought. That's because the lens on a point-and-shoot camera, especially a fixed (non-zoom) lens, is deliberately designed to provide the maximum possible depth of field – the rationale being that for holiday and similar snaps most people will want their images to be sharp all the way from the foreground to the background.

However, with advanced compacts and dSLRs, you can control the depth of field so that a selected area of the image, whether foreground,

Aperture priority

The safest way to experiment with depth of field is to set the camera to Aperture priority (A/Av). In this semi-automatic mode, you can alter the aperture setting, and thus change the depth of field, knowing that the camera will adjust the shutter speed automatically, and/or the ISO setting (when set to Auto) to ensure you still get an accurately exposed image.

background or the middle distance, is in focus. Selective focus is a key element in more advanced photography.

Aperture

Let's look in more detail at the factors that control depth of field; there are essentially three.

The first and most obvious factor determining depth of field is the aperture. It's been impossible to avoid any discussion of how the size of a lens's aperture affects depth of field as they are so closely related. But to reinforce the concept here, a large aperture (small number, such as f/2.8) will create a small or narrow depth of field, while a small aperture (large number, such as f/16) will create a large or wide depth of field. Because the amount of available light has a direct impact on the aperture setting (in other words the amount of light that reaches the sensor), it therefore follows that the amount of available light also has some impact on depth of field. For example, in low-light conditions (assuming an ISO setting of 100), the only way to achieve a wide depth of field (using a small aperture of f/11) would be to have a long exposure of, say, 2 sec or longer, in which case you'll certainly need a tripod. The opposite happens in very bright conditions, where the only way to achieve a very

narrow depth of field (using a large aperture of f/2.8) would be to have an extremely fast shutter speed of, say, $^1/_{4000}$ or even $^1/_{8000}$ sec. Many cameras don't have those fast shutter speeds, so the only way to achieve such a shot would be to use dark filters over the lens to restrict the light striking the sensor. Although extreme, these examples illustrate why it's so important to familiarize yourself with your camera's manual controls so that you can achieve the shots you want in the conditions that are available to you.

Focal length

The second factor affecting depth of field is the focal length of the lens. Wide-angle settings on zoom lenses (such as 28mm) provide greater depth of field at the same aperture setting than telephoto lenses or telephoto settings (such as 200mm). We won't go into the optical rules that make this so, but it's important to understand how depth of field is affected by focal length so that you can begin to 'previsualize' the results you can expect from varying focal lengths. Having done so, you will then begin to make considered judgements about how different lenses or zoom settings can achieve different creative results. There's

Focus on middle tree   **Focus on nearest tree**

certainly more to focal length then simply getting 'closer' or 'farther away' from your subject.

Focusing distance

The final factor that determines depth of field is the distance between the subject and the lens. The closer the subject is to the lens the narrower the depth of field. As the subject moves farther away from the lens the depth of field increases, up to a point where – depending on the focal length of the lens and the aperture setting – everything beyond will be in focus. This is often referred to as 'infinity' (∞).

APERTURE

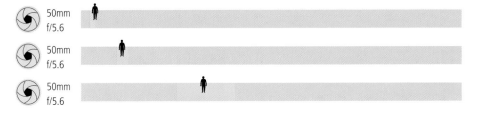

50mm f/1.4

50mm f/5.6

50mm f/16

LEFT Changing the size of the lens aperture radically alters the amount of the scene, from foreground to background, which is captured in focus (represented by the yellow blocks). The wider the aperture (the smaller the number), the less of the scene is in focus.

FOCAL LENGTH

28mm f/5.6

50mm f/5.6

200mm f/5.6

LEFT The second factor affecting depth of field is focal length. As the diagram shows, the longer the focal length (shown in millimetres), the narrower the depth of field. Compare the wide-angle (28mm) lens with the telephoto (200mm) lens.

FOCUSING DISTANCE

50mm f/5.6

50mm f/5.6

50mm f/5.6

LEFT Finally, distance affects depth of field, although compared with the other two factors, the variation is much smaller. With the same focal length lens set at the same aperture, depth of field increases the farther the subject is from the camera.

Wide Depth of Field

Landscape photography springs to mind most readily when we think of wide depth of field, with photographers traditionally aiming to ensure that the zone of sharpness is as great as possible.

Sweeping views

For broad, sweeping, pin-sharp landscape views choose a wide-angle lens or zoom setting (around 28mm is appropriate) and 'close' the aperture down as far as it will go – in other words set the aperture to its smallest opening (highest 'f' number). The most appropriate mode for controlling the aperture setting is, unsurprisingly, the Aperture priority (A/Av) mode. If possible, place the camera on a tripod or a stable surface and select the camera's self-timer; alternatively use a shutter-release cable or remote shutter release.

ABOVE A wide depth of field coupled with a wide-angle view can be used to good effect to show scenes from unusual viewpoints.

Next, frame the shot, focusing a third of the way into the image (see Hyperfocal distance box), which should provide you with the deepest possible depth of field. Using both a tripod and self-timer/remote or cable shutter release will ensure that the camera is as stable as possible when the shutter actually fires. This is particularly important in low-lighting conditions when the shutter speed may be a relatively slow $1/15$ sec or $1/30$ sec. Fixing the camera to the tripod and then using your finger to press the shutter release is somewhat self-defeating as you're likely to shake the camera, although only by a tiny fraction, which can soften the image.

Review

Once you've taken the shot, review the principal elements of the image to check that they're sharp. You may want to make adjustments to the point of focus depending on which parts of the image are more significant. If the foreground plays a more important role in the composition than the background for example, you'll want the foreground to be sharper than the background.

HYPERFOCAL DISTANCE

One technique employed by all professional landscape photographers is hyperfocal focusing. This works on the basis that when you focus on a subject, a third of the scene in front will be in focus, while two-thirds behind will also be in focus – the point of focus is known as the hyperfocal distance. Focusing here will give you the maximum possible depth of field. There exist fairly complex charts (www.dofmaster.com) that will tell you exactly what the hyperfocal distance will be for a given focal length at a specific aperture.

However, an easier, if not absolutely accurate way to find the hyperfocal distance is to focus manually a third of the way into the scene. This will give you maximum depth of field.

ABOVE By focusing at the hyperfocal distance, everything from foreground to background is sharp in this shot.

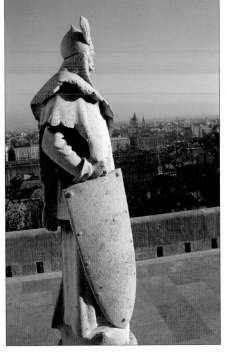

If you don't have a tripod or anything on which to rest the camera when shooting landscapes, check that, having set the aperture, the shutter speed is sufficiently fast to prevent camera shake. You may need to increase either the aperture slightly or the ISO setting to get a suitably fast shutter speed. You'll find yourself increasingly making this sort of compromise the more you take control of the camera. But doing it manually, rather than letting the camera choose the settings, means you're the one making the important decisions; and if you don't get the image you want when you come to preview it, you'll have a better idea about how to improve it.

ABOVE Ensuring that the path from the bottom of the image is sharp has helped to reinforce it as a leading line.

ABOVE Keeping the view of Budapest in focus in the distance helps to reinforce the relationship between the statue and the city.

ABOVE When using wide depth of field with a wide-angle lens in landscape photography, it's natural to want to include the horizon and sky. But remember, this can lead the viewer's eye out of the image. To contain the viewer in the picture, dispense with the horizon and sky. In the second image (right), by excluding the sky our attention remains much more focused on the bay and the picturesque town.

LEFT By including some sharply focused foliage in the foreground, the photographer has added a sense of depth and scale to this view of the Art Deco district of Miami.

Narrow Depth of Field

Deliberately throwing regions of an image out of focus might seem counterintuitive, particularly if you're used to a point-and-shoot camera that is designed to keep as much of the scene as possible in focus. However, being able to select which parts of an image are in focus and which are blurred is a fundamental aspect of creative photography and is often referred to as differential focus.

In the discussion on compositional balance in Chapter 2, we learned that an in-focus element attracts our attention much more than one that is out of focus. Photographers can use this to their advantage in a variety of situations by keeping depth of field down to a narrow margin.

Portraits

One genre of photography where restricting depth of field is often critical is portraiture. The ability to throw a potentially distracting background or foreground out of focus is the key to many successful

portrait shots, as it concentrates the viewer's attention on the subject of the image. The most effective way to obtain a narrow, or shallow, depth of field – so that only the subject is in focus – is to start with a telephoto lens or zoom setting between 100mm and 300mm. This is because telephoto lenses have a narrower depth of field

ABOVE Using narrow depth of field has thrown this group of people out of focus, so we get a sense of time and place rather than focusing on the individuals themselves.

than wide-angle lenses, making it easier to throw backgrounds out of focus. Then, in Aperture priority (A/Av) mode, 'open up' the lens by selecting the largest aperture setting (smallest 'f' number). You'll find that this is exactly what the camera does automatically if you select Portrait mode. Having selected the largest aperture, make sure that the shutter speed is sufficiently fast to prevent camera shake. This is particularly important with longer focal length lenses or zoom settings, as these are more prone to suffering from camera shake because slight movement is exaggerated over distance. Position yourself at an appropriate distance from the subject so that just the head and shoulders are in the frame and fire the

LEFT Using a narrow, or shallow, depth of field can make a background less distracting, so the main subject stands out.

◀ **LEFT** A narrow, or shallow, depth of field helps the viewer to focus on the main subject of an image – in this case the baby.

▼ **BELOW** We know what the subject of this picture is, despite most of it being blurred, but this adds to the creative effect.

▲ **ABOVE** As depth of field decreases the closer you are to your subject, there's a very narrow depth of field in macro photography.

shutter. When reviewing the image, you should find that the subject is nice and sharp and that the foreground and/or background is so out of focus that your eye glosses over them.

Evidently, it's not just portraiture photography that can benefit from controlling depth of field. Narrow depth of field has its place in just about all genres of photography, especially when it comes to nature and art photography. Later on in this chapter we shall be looking in more detail at close-up and macro photography, where a narrow depth of field can be particularly effective with shots of insects and flowers, or any small object photographed close up.

BOKEH

As your skill at controlling depth of field and using differential focus increases, you'll become aware of blurry hexagonal shapes, particularly in highlights. These are created by the shape of the lens's aperture blades as they close down to the aperture setting, and are called 'bokeh', the Japanese word for 'blur'.

Bokeh is a subjective aesthetic quality, but the general consensus is that the smoother and more circular the bokeh, the more pleasing the out-of-focus area. Much relies on the lens quality, and as such is out of your control. However, by adjusting the aperture you can control the amount by which the background is thrown out of focus, thus controlling the size of the bokeh highlights.

▲ **ABOVE** 'Bokeh' are the circular, defocused highlights seen in the right of the image.

Depth of Field – Try It Yourself

Having covered the theory of controlling depth of field and armed with a knowledge of how to maximize or minimize the zone of sharpness, it's time to put that knowledge into practice. The exercises below are much easier to carry out, and the results more apparent, if you use a tripod, but it's not essential.

Increasing depth of field

Let's begin by learning how to increase depth of field, or the zone of sharpness. Place three objects about 24in (60cm) apart in a line on a long table. Size is not an issue, but apples and oranges are an appropriate size. Set the camera on the tripod about 3ft (1m) from the front object, but slightly higher and off to one side. Now, adjust the zoom lens so that the front object almost fills the viewfinder and the other two objects are still visible.

Focus on the lead object and select the largest aperture (smallest number) setting your camera lens has (for example, f/2.8). Take a photo and review it. You should find that only the lead object is in focus, while the other two are out of focus, with the rear object more out of focus than the middle one. Now, close the aperture down by about 3 stops (to f/8 in our example) and take another shot. On reviewing the second shot, the first two objects should now be in focus, but the final one still out of focus. Finally, close the lens right down (to f/22, for example). The final shot should feature all of your objects sharply in focus.

RIGHT By controlling the depth of field so that both the foreground and background in this image are out of focus, our eyes are immediately drawn to the subject of the shot.

Focal length

As we know, adjusting a lens's focal length also impacts on depth of field. For this next exercise, take the camera off the tripod if you've been using one. Set the aperture to f/4 and set the camera lens to its longest focal length (in other words zoom right into the first object, but make sure the other two objects are still visible), and take a picture, but from a slightly higher position than previously. Then set the lens to its shortest focal length (zoom out), but move closer to the objects so that the first one still fills the frame, and take another shot.

When comparing these two images, you should be able to see how the zone of sharpness is greater with the shorter focal length setting. It should also be apparent how the longer focal length has foreshortened the distance between the three objects. When we look at focal length we'll discover how this foreshortening effect can be used to our advantage.

Selective focus

In this next exercise, we're going to selectively focus on one of the three objects. Simply set the aperture to f/4, focus on the first object and take a shot. Next, focus on the centre object and take a shot, and then do the same with the rear object. When you review your shots you should find that each object in turn is sharp while the other two remain blurred. This is an excellent way of placing emphasis on specific elements in a scene.

Real world

Next time you're out and about with a camera, look to repeat the exercises above, but on a larger scale, such as with a line of trees. At larger scales the differential focus should be more apparent, and you should start to get a feel for how controlling depth of field can be used in your real-world photography.

 ABOVE RIGHT This sequence of three images shows how closing down the aperture increases depth of field. Compare the zone of sharpness from f/2.8 with that from f/22.

RIGHT These three images demonstrate how effective selective focus can be at drawing the viewer's eye to a particular part or element of a scene.

Longest focal length

Shortest focal length

 LEFT These two images demonstrate the effect of focal length on depth of field. The first image shows a narrower zone of sharpness compared with the second (compare the walls at the end of the room). But also note how in the first image the three objects appear much closer together than in the second – this is because longer focal lengths foreshorten the distance between objects.

f/2.8   **f/8**   **f/22**

Focus on first object   **Focus on centre object**   **Focus on rear object**

Shutter Speed

Along with the aperture setting, shutter speed is the other factor that governs how much light reaches the camera's sensor. The faster the shutter speed, the less time the sensor is exposed to light. Shutter speeds are usually measured in fractions of a second (sec), although much longer exposures are sometimes used, and historically each setting is either half or double the next. For example, a typical digital camera may have the following shutter speeds: $1/1000$ sec; $1/500$ sec; $1/250$ sec; $1/125$ sec; $1/60$ sec; $1/30$ sec; $1/15$ sec; $1/8$ sec; $1/4$ sec; $1/2$ sec; 1 sec; 2 sec; 4 sec; 8 sec, 15 sec and 30 sec. More sophisticated cameras may have a wider range, featuring faster shutter speeds of $1/2000$ sec, $1/4000$ sec and $1/8000$ sec, or include $1/2$-stop or $1/3$-stop 'intermediary' speeds such as $1/80$ sec or $1/100$ sec.

Shutter speed: $1/60$ sec

Shutter speed: $1/125$ sec

Camera shake

When deciding on the shutter speed to use, particularly with 'hand-held' photography, try to ensure that you select a shutter speed that is fast enough to prevent 'camera shake'. Camera shake occurs when the camera moves while the shutter is open, resulting in a blurred image. Depending on the focal length of the lens or the zoom setting, different shutter speeds are needed in order to avoid camera shake. For example, with a short (wide-angle) focal length setting of 28mm, a shutter speed of $1/30$ sec should be fast enough to prevent camera shake, but with a long

▲ **ABOVE** This sequence of images clearly shows how increasing shutter speed freezes movement. Compare the slowest shutter speed ($1/60$ sec) with the fastest ($1/1000$ sec).

(telephoto) focal length setting of 200mm, you'll need a shutter speed of $1/250$ sec. This is because the longer the focal length; the more camera shake becomes apparent.

Minimum shutter speeds

As a rule of thumb, to prevent camera shake the shutter speed should be close to the reciprocal of the focal length of the lens. For example, if the focal length is 60mm the shutter

◀ **FAR LEFT** In this shot a tripod was used with an exposure of around 1 sec. This way the buildings and stalls remained sharp but the bustling crowd blurred.

◀ **LEFT** This deliberately blurred shot was hand held with a shutter speed of around $1/15$ sec. The blurred effect conveys the pace of city life.

Shutter speed: $^1/_{250}$ sec

Shutter speed: $^1/_{500}$ sec

...

Shutter speed: $^1/_{1000}$ sec

speed should be a minimum of $^1/_{60}$ sec, while a focal length of 125mm requires a shutter speed of at least $^1/_{125}$ sec and a 500mm focal length needs $^1/_{500}$ sec. Remember, however, these are only guidelines and they won't guarantee that you'll get sharp pictures every time.

In addition to using the minimum shutter speed as described above, try leaning against a solid support, such as a wall or tree, and gently squeeze the shutter release rather than 'press' it. Some professionals, whenever they're shooting hand held, set their camera's drive or shooting mode to 'continuous' and fire off three or four shots so that they can select the sharpest image from the set. Of course, by doing this, you'll use up far more memory, but if it's an important shot and you're worried about potential camera shake, it is certainly an option to consider.

Alternatively, you can increase the ISO sensitivity setting to obtain a faster shutter speed. As we know, the more sensitive the camera's sensor is to light, the less time the sensor needs to be exposed to the light from the scene being photographed. Each incremental ISO setting allows you to halve the shutter speed. So, if you're worried about camera shake at $^1/_{30}$ sec at ISO 100, set the ISO to 200

and you can set the shutter speed to $^1/_{60}$ sec, or use ISO 400 for a shutter speed of $^1/_{125}$ sec.

Shutter speed and exposure

The shutter speed chosen for a specific shot also plays a role in determining how an image will look – whether, for example, motion is blurred or frozen, or whether the image has a wide or narrow zone of sharpness. This latter is due to the relationship between the shutter speed and aperture setting.

For example, the lack of a tripod in low-light conditions may well need a fast shutter speed of, say, $^1/_{125}$ sec. Such a fast shutter speed in low-light situations will need a wide aperture to allow more light to reach the sensor, and the wider the aperture the narrower the depth of field.

Over the next few pages, we'll look at when slow or fast shutter speeds are appropriate, their effect on your images, and how shutter speed can be used creatively for artistic effect.

IMAGE STABILIZATION

Some cameras and individual lenses for dSLRs have image-stabilization (IS) systems. These work in a variety of ways, but generally they feature gyroscopic motors that detect and counteract any movement in the camera or lens. The systems vary in how successful they are, but generally you can expect to reduce the shutter speed by 2–3 stops and still retain sharp images. For example, if you had selected a shutter speed of $^1/_{250}$ sec without image stabilization, with image stabilization enabled you would be able to shoot with a speed as slow as $^1/_{60}$ sec (or even $^1/_{30}$ sec) and still get blur-free results.

IS off

IS on

Fast Shutter Speeds

Shutter speeds of around $^{1}/_{250}$ sec and shorter are generally considered fast. With the most commonly used focal lengths ranging from around 40mm to 125mm, using fast shutter speeds should certainly prevent camera shake. In fact, speeds of $^{1}/_{500}$ sec and shorter will freeze fast-moving action beyond the perception of the human eye.

Freezing action

Ever since the 19th-century English photographer, Eadweard Muybridge, shot his famous sequence of a horse galloping, we have been fascinated with the ability to freeze photographs of fast-moving action.

The actual shutter speed required to arrest movement very much depends on the direction the object is moving. A speeding car heading toward the camera, for example, won't require as fast a shutter speed as someone walking across the viewfinder or something moving directly up or down in front of the camera. In addition to the direction of movement, the distance of the object from the camera and the focal length of the lens are also critical factors. The farther the

object is from the camera, and the shorter the focal length, the slower the shutter speed can be before action is frozen. Or in other words, the farther away a fast-moving object is, the slower it appears to move.

However, for sports photography, when you're likely to be using the longest focal length setting available on the lens, such as 300mm, in order to get optically as 'close' as you can to the action, speeds of around $^{1}/_{1000}$ sec are probably necessary to freeze the action. At these shutter speeds it's

▲ **ABOVE** A shutter speed of $^{1}/_{400}$ sec has been used to make sure the surfer and the water are 'frozen'.

▼ **BELOW** A fast-moving subject that is travelling across the frame requires a fast shutter speed to prevent blur – in this instance $^{1}/_{620}$ sec.

likely you'll need to use the lens's widest aperture setting to get a correct exposure, and unless the lighting conditions are very bright you may need to increase the ISO.

Fast-motion freezing

In order to freeze motion you need to make sure you've set a shutter speed that's fast enough, so follow this guide:
• Subjects moving across the frame need a faster shutter speed than subjects moving toward (or away from) the camera.
• Use the Shutter Priority (S/Tv) mode in order to control the shutter speed, and let the camera select the aperture.

LEFT Fast-moving subjects moving toward the camera don't necessarily need as fast a shutter speed as a subject moving across the frame, but here a shutter speed of $^1/_{500}$ sec was used to freeze the action.

Shutter priority

The best way to experiment with shutter speeds is to select the Shutter Priority setting (S/Tv), choose an appropriate shutter speed, then focus on an area where the action will take place. Check in the viewfinder to see if an underexposure warning is flashing. If it is, you'll either need to increase the ISO setting until an acceptable exposure is available or, if that still doesn't provide the correct exposure, reduce the shutter speed slightly as well.

RIGHT Although the photographer has used a sufficiently fast shutter speed to capture this beautiful shot of a hummingbird hawk moth, its wings are beating so fast that even a very fast shutter speed of $^1/_{1000}$ sec can't freeze their movement.

LEFT Although moving across the image, the horses are still relatively small in the frame, allowing $^1/_{320}$ sec to be used for this action shot.

Standard Shutter Speeds

For most hand-held photography, shutter speeds of between $^1/_{30}$ sec and $^1/_{250}$ sec are most commonly used. At these speeds, images that are captured tend to replicate our perception of the world around us, so some parts of a scene will be sharply in focus, while more rapidly moving elements may appear slightly blurred.

The essence of speed

While on one level it's interesting to look at images that freeze time, there are occasions when freezing an object entirely can detract from the sense of action, especially if the background is also frozen. An obvious example is high-speed motor sport, in which a racing car or motorbike, if captured with a fast shutter speed, can look static and lose the sense of speed.

▼ **BELOW** Not all images have to be pin sharp. The slow shutter speed used in this hand-held urban shot provides a sense of movement and adds to the atmosphere of the image.

Deliberate blur

There are two ways to stop action shots appearing static and dull, both of which involve deliberately introducing blur. The first method is to select a slower shutter speed than you would usually use to freeze the action. Begin around 3 stops slower, so set $^1/_{30}$ sec instead of $^1/_{250}$ sec, for example, then prefocus on an area into which you know the subject will enter and take the shot as it enters the frame. If the subject is relatively stationary, for example a golfer, simply take the shot using the slower shutter speed. The result will be a blurred, or partly blurred, subject in front of a sharp background (or foreground). Depending on the amount of blur and the subject matter this may evoke the sense of action you need. The golfer is a good example, as ideally the head, shoulders and legs should remain relatively still and therefore sharp while the arms and club form a blurred arc.

Panning

For many types of action photography, and in particular fast-moving sports photography, the danger with the technique described previously is that the sharp background becomes the focus of attention, while the blurred subject – especially if it's entirely blurred with nothing sharply in focus – will not attract the viewer's eye. To overcome this, try using the well-known technique called 'panning'. Ensure that your feet are well planted and hold the camera to your eye. Frame the subject of the shot and by turning your body from the waist up only, follow the subject through the viewfinder. As the subject passes, take a shot, using your camera's continuous shooting mode if it has one. Continue to turn

▼ **BELOW** For subjects that are moving across the frame, panning is a great way of showing speed. Just follow the subject with the camera as it moves.

Framing

It takes time to learn how to pan successfully. Don't start by zooming close in to the subject so it fills the frame, as any error will result in part of the subject being cut off. Instead, zoom out a bit to give yourself a better chance and crop away excess background later if required. Also, start by trying to get the subject in the centre of the frame, so you're less likely to cut the front or back off the subject. As you become more proficient, try zooming in with a longer focal length lens or setting to get 'closer' to the subject and framing the shot so that there is more space in front of it than behind. Moving subjects look better if there's space in the frame into which they can move.

your upper torso and track the subject as it moves out of view, while you are making the exposure. You'll find that you can probably only comfortably turn through around 45°, but the result should be a sharp subject in front of a blurred background. This will not only give you a sense of speed, but it will also show a well-focused subject that holds the viewer's attention.

When panning, select the same shutter speed as in the previous technique – that is around 4 stops less than necessary to freeze the action (between $1/30$ sec and $1/125$ sec usually works for most sports). If it's possible, also try to position yourself in front of a background that features a lot of light and dark tones, as these will make the blurred effect more apparent.

▲ **TOP** Slow shutter speeds can be used to add a sense of movement to landscapes. Here the waves have become a 'mist' thanks to the use of a slow shutter speed.

◀ **LEFT** A wide-angle lens has increased the dramatic perspective here, while a slow shutter speed records the snowball hurtling toward the photographer as a blur.

Long Exposures

Although most photographs are taken using shutter speeds of a fraction of a second, most advanced digital cameras have the facility to shoot much longer exposures – anywhere between 1 and 30 seconds. Some cameras also feature a 'Bulb' (B) setting, which keeps the shutter open for as long as the shutter release is held down (or until the battery runs out). But when would you use such long exposures?

ZOOM BURST

If your camera has a manual zoom control, try creating a 'zoom burst'. With the camera on a tripod, select the smallest aperture and a slow ISO setting to obtain a long shutter speed – anything from around ¼ sec to ½ sec or longer is sufficient. Focus on an area that contains a mix of light and dark tones and centre it in the viewfinder. With the lens zoomed in, set the camera's self-timer and press the shutter release. When you hear the shutter fire, gently twist the zoom control so the lens zooms out. The result should be an abstract zoom burst.

Low light

Normally, exposures of a second or more are used in low light, where you won't be able to hand-hold the camera and still obtain sharp images. To start with, you'll need to use a tripod, or at least rest the camera on a sturdy support, to avoid blurry night-time (or early morning) shots. Also, use either the camera's self-timer, a shutter release cable or a remote control so you don't run the risk of moving the camera with your finger while firing the shutter.

Because the camera is mounted on a stable platform it's not necessary to set a high ISO setting, so set the ISO to the lowest setting available to produce less noisy images. In addition, use the camera's noise-reduction setting.

Some of the most effective extended exposures taken during night-time – especially in towns and cities – show the trails made by the lights of passing cars. Find a vantage point overlooking a busy thoroughfare, set the camera on a tripod, and experiment with a variety of long exposure times.

RIGHT Use a long exposure to record several fireworks in a single frame for eye-catching shots such as this one.

ABOVE Shooting indoors using a slow shutter speed to get an appropriate exposure has resulted in blurred figures, which add to the movement of this photograph.

Trails made by stars can also create effective long-exposure images. For these, you'll probably need to use the camera's Bulb setting as exposures often have to be several minutes long, if not longer, to chart the progress of the stars. For best results, choose a clear night that's free of cloud and other ambient light, and experiment with the length of your exposures.

ABOVE For this night-time cityscape, a long shutter speed was essential to record the beautifully lit buildings. With shots like these, a tripod is essential.

Extended daytime exposures

It's not just at night that you can use long exposures for creative effect. Certain daytime scenes also benefit from extended exposures, especially scenes featuring flowing water, mist or low-lying cloud. The long exposure will smooth out the water or cloud so it appears as a soft, nebulous mass.

Because of the relatively high light levels present during the day, the smallest aperture and lowest ISO settings might not allow you to set a suitably long exposure, so you'll have to reduce the amount of light reaching the sensor some other way. To do this you'll need to use a neutral density (ND) filter. These filters work a bit like sunglasses in that they reduce the amount of light hitting the sensor, but they don't affect the colour of the light – hence 'neutral' density.

WHITE BALANCE

Because most extended exposures are shot at night, and many are city- or townscapes, you'll instantly become aware of the colour cast created by sodium, tungsten and mercury vapour lights. If there is a sufficient variety of lighting in the shot, it may add to the effect of the image, but a dull overall orange cast simply looks unpleasant, as shown in the image below left.

In such instances, it's likely that the camera's Auto White Balance won't be able to address the problem, and you'll need to resort to fixing the colour cast using image-editing software to bring back the whites, or by setting a manual white balance if your camera has this option available.

Auto White Balance

Corrected White Balance

Creative Exposure

Armed with a better understanding of the concept of exposure, how the various metering systems operate and how to use the camera's manual settings, you should now feel much more confident to experiment with exposure settings. As sophisticated as your camera's matrix or evaluative metering system is, and as tempting as it is to let the camera work out the shutter speed/aperture setting for you, you're really missing out on producing some great shots if you let the camera do all the work. The beauty of shooting digitally is that experimenting with seemingly 'inaccurate' exposures doesn't cost a thing, apart from a bit of battery power. If you don't like an image, simply delete it and start again. There's nothing to lose by experimenting a little, and nothing to be gained if you don't.

Light

Often, the difference between an average shot and one that attracts a little more attention is the quality of light and the relationship between the light and dark areas. You may find that if you leave the decision about the exposure to the camera, it will attempt to set an exposure that ensures detail is visible in both highlight and shadow regions. Of course, in many cases this is absolutely the right course of action, but if the interplay of light and dark areas is the key to the image, rather than specific detail, it's time to override the camera and experiment with different exposures.

BELOW LEFT This is a well-exposed floral study enhanced by the backlighting and the lone pink flower in a sea of blue and green.

BELOW RIGHT The same shot as the one on the left, but this time a longer shutter speed has been used, and the camera moved during the exposure. The result is an abstract blur of colour that creates an entirely different effect to the first picture.

OPPOSITE There's absolutely nothing 'wrong' with the exposure for this building, but the exposure has retained all the shadow areas, and it appears to be lacking contrast.

BELOW Here the exposure has been adjusted slightly, so the scene is a little darker than the first one. Deepening the shadows makes the windows stand out more for a dramatic effect.

You may find that deliberately under-exposing a shot brings richer tone and colour to the highlight areas, and although the shadows may 'fill in' a little, so detail becomes less visible, the viewer is struck more by the contrast between light and shade. Similarly, there may be times when overexposing an image, so that many of the highlight areas are 'blown out', has more impact and evokes a greater impression of heat, light or even space than an accurately exposed image.

Movement

As we've discovered over the last few pages, you can use shutter speeds to bring a creative touch to an image – either fast shutter speeds to freeze fast-moving action or slow shutter speeds to generate a sense of movement in an image. With longer shutter speeds, general wisdom suggests that you use a tripod to avoid camera shake, so ensuring that your images are pin sharp. However, images don't always have to be sharply focused to be successful. People have experimented by deliberately moving the camera when the shutter is open in all sorts of ways to see what results can be achieved, a process known as 'kinetic photography'. The on-line photography site Flickr (www.flickr.com) even has a group called 'Camera Toss', which demonstrates the results you can achieve from simply throwing your camera in the air during an exposure of $1/2$ sec or longer.

While going to such extremes with an expensive camera may not be advisable, there's absolutely nothing to stop you from setting a very slow shutter speed and moving or waving your camera around to see the results. Bear in mind that it's best to try such exposures in front of a scene that has contrasting tones or colours, as that way the movement will be more apparent. There are countless ways to experiment with light and movement with a camera, and while a lot of the time the results may not come to much, every now

TOP Using the camera's evaluative/multi-segment metering pattern gives a nice record shot of this scene, and it wouldn't look out of place in a holiday album.

ABOVE By overexposing a similar photograph, we have a shot that's fit for exhibiting. The overexposure has helped to blur the tonal distinction between the foreground sand and the sky in the background. This focuses our attention on the middle of the frame – the strip of blue water in which the subjects of the image can be found.

and again you'll end up creating an image that will be unique, personal and striking.

Exposure – Try It Yourself

You should by now have a better understanding of the relationship between shutter and aperture, and having run through the 'depth of field' exercises, be more confident with your camera's semi-automatic and manual settings.

The exercises here will help to reinforce your familiarity with the camera's aperture and shutter controls, and also get you to think about how adjusting exposure can introduce atmosphere into an image, or create a sense of movement. Unlike the 'depth of field' exercises, which dealt with how the mechanics and optical properties of the camera and its lens can be used specifically to draw attention to certain elements of an image, these exercises are far more subjective, and the final results will be very personal to you.

Controlling light levels

First, reacquaint yourself with the camera's controls. Having a tripod and a form of remote shutter release will make life easier, but they are not essential. Try this exercise outdoors, using objects and a setting that exhibit good tonal variation – such as a dark object on a light table.

Set your camera to its Manual mode, select a medium aperture (such as f/8), and a focal length of 100mm. Look through the viewfinder, focus on an object 16ft (5m) away, ensuring that you can see regions in front of and behind the object. Adjust the shutter speed until the exposure level indicator is set to '0', and fire the shutter. Now reduce the shutter speed 2 stops (from say $^1/_{500}$ sec to $^1/_{125}$ sec) and increase the aperture to compensate (from f/8 to f/16). The exposure indicator should still read '0'. Fire another shot and compare the two images. You should see little or no difference in the overall exposure, but the second image should have a wider zone of sharpness – as we would expect having completed the 'depth of field' exercises.

Next, having reduced the shutter speed, don't increase the aperture to compensate. The exposure level indicator should read around '-2' – take a shot. Increase the shutter speed 2 stops (the level should read around '0'), but reduce the aperture by 2 stops to take the reading back down to around '-2' again. These last two shots will be underexposed by 2 stops, but look closely, first at the overall tones of the images. Although the darker areas are likely to be underexposed, the lighter tones may well have become richer and easier to define, and where colour is present these tones may appear more saturated. This is because the lighter an image is, the less saturated the colours. When comparing the zone of sharpness between the two images, the second image should show a wider depth of field.

Carry on experimenting with the exposure settings so that you underexpose by 1 stop and overexpose by 1

Aperture: f/8

Aperture: f/16

Underexposed by 1 stop

Underexposed by 2 stops

LEFT Different but correct exposure variations result in the same overall exposure, but both images at the top have greater depth of field; the underexposed images have richer colours.

¹/₃₀ **sec shutter speed**

¹/₆₀ **sec shutter speed**

¹/₁₂₅ **sec shutter speed**

¹/₂₅₀ **sec shutter speed**

¹/₅₀₀ **sec shutter speed**

¹/₁₀₀₀ **sec shutter speed**

and 2 stops. Compare the images to see how over- and underexposure affect tones and colours.

Controlling blur

Using a focal length of about 50mm, set the camera to Shutter Priority (S/Tv). Begin with a slow shutter speed (¹/₃₀ sec) and ask a friend to run in front of the camera at approximately 10ft (3m) from the lens. When your subject appears in the viewfinder take a shot. Repeat the exercise, increasing the shutter speed by 1 stop each time. By around ¹/₅₀₀ sec most of the movement should be frozen, and by ¹/₁₀₀₀ sec the figure

ABOVE AND RIGHT The simple exercise described here shows you how shutter speed controls sense of movement. Although it's tempting and seems natural to use a fast shutter to freeze fast action, this may result in a static-looking image.

should be entirely sharp. Reduce the shutter speed to ¹/₃₀ sec and focus on your friend as he or she begins to run forward. Start panning and fire the shutter when your friend moves directly in front of you. Continue to pan as the exposure is made and the image should show your subject more or less frozen, but the background should be blurred.

Panning

Tonal Contrast

The vast majority of us have an inherent understanding of how a high-contrast image and a low-contrast one differ. However, it's important to understand what factors make an image exhibit a high or low degree of contrast, so that you can quickly spot high- or low-contrast situations in order to make the most of them.

High contrast

Essentially, images that are comprised of very dark and light tones, with little in between, are referred to as high-contrast images. In fact, many of us still most closely associate high-contrast images with black and white photography. However, the juxtaposition of the tones can also influence our perception of how much contrast there is in an image. If, for example, dark and light tones sit next to one another, then the image appears to have higher contrast

than if the dark and light tones are separated by more neutral tones, even though the overall tonal content is similar. In this respect, it's the subject that determines the contrast of the photograph.

Lighting

A second factor that contributes to contrast is lighting. If you fold a piece of paper continually back and forth to make a zigzag shape, then lay it on the surface of the table and light it from above, it appears almost continuous in tone with very little contrast. But shine a light from the side

and the shadows created by the ridges of the paper make the surface appear almost black and white.

Silhouettes

By their very nature, silhouettes are the most extreme form of high-contrast shots. Placing the subject against a light background and then exposing for the background will ensure that all detail within the subject is severely underexposed, leaving just the outline.

Silhouettes have passed out of fashion slightly for being somewhat clichéd, but they can still create

ABOVE The contrast in this shot doesn't come from the lighting, but from the subject – in this case the light and dark curves of the water.

LEFT Silhouettes work best when the background is much lighter than the subject. Here the sun acts as the back-ground, turning the trees black.

some powerful, atmospheric images. Remember to pick your subject carefully for its shape, rather than its form. Always bear in mind that you will not only lose the subject's form but pretty much all of its colour, too.

Low contrast

Shots that are said to be 'low contrast' rely on the image's neutral tones graduating into one another, creating a calm, gentle atmosphere. We tend to associate low-contrast images with hazy distant hills, the soft, shadowless lighting you get before the sun has risen or after it has set, or on a cloudy day – all conditions that the majority of photographers don't like because everything appears dull and flat. But striking images can be found under such circumstances – it's simply a case of finding subjects that emphasize the serene, tranquil and ethereal nature.

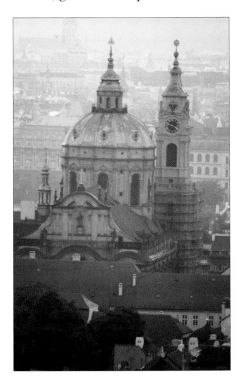

TOP Taken just before sunrise, the light in the sky is diffuse and soft, resulting in a low-contrast image. However, this suits landscape photographs, as does the light at the end of the day.

ABOVE RIGHT Hard lighting that gives a high-contrast result suits strong graphic shapes, such as this detail of a park bench.

LEFT Soft, diffused lighting created by an early misty morning will even out colour variation and create a low-contrast scene.

RIGHT Hard, directional lighting produces bright highlights and deep shadows – perfect for the shiny, silvery scales of these fish. The result is an almost monochrome high-contrast image.

Colour Contrast

Although we usually think of tone as a decisive element that dictates whether an image exhibits high or low contrast, determined by the presence and juxtaposition of light and dark tones, there is another factor that determines our perception of contrast – colour. In the same way that tonal variation can determine the contrast in black and white images, colour variation can have the same effect in colour photography.

High colour contrast

Later we'll look in more detail at the emotions that certain colours can elicit and the effect of colour saturation, but here we're going to concentrate on how colour can be used to augment or reduce contrast, and the impact that it has on the viewer.

When closely juxtaposed, colours that lie opposite one another on the colour wheel, such as cold blues and warm reds, create a high-contrast effect and, as with high tonal contrast, this adds dynamism to an image. When using colour in this way, the most important thing is to ensure that the colour in the image is the main

Colour wheel

Colours that occupy adjacent areas on the colour wheel create a calming, low-contrast effect, while those that sit opposite each other add high-contrast drama to a picture.

subject. In many ways it's irrelevant if the subject is unrecognizable, as the response you're aiming to get from the viewer is triggered by the colour,

▼ **BELOW LEFT** These umbrellas provide a high colour-contrasting image, helped by the fact that the orange and blue sit almost opposite one another on the colour wheel.

▼ **BELOW RIGHT** The reds and oranges of these fruits create a strong colour contrast when seen against the green leaves and blue sky beyond.

rather than by the subject. The best way to explore high colour contrast is to look for subjects that feature only two colours, that are ideally situated opposite one another on the colour wheel. The impact will be greater if you zoom in as much as possible to exclude any other potentially distracting objects or colours.

Low colour contrast

Colours that share similar regions of the colour wheel create low colour contrast, and have a soothing or calming effect. The same applies to images that are made up primarily of only one colour (although this can vary depending on the colour).

The principal difference between high and low colour contrast is that with the former it's the colours, or rather the juxtaposition of the colours, that evokes the viewer's response, whereas with low colour contrast, the image needs to feature additional compositional elements in order for it to work successfully. Elements such as texture, form or even subtle tonal differences will all help to reinforce the colour harmony.

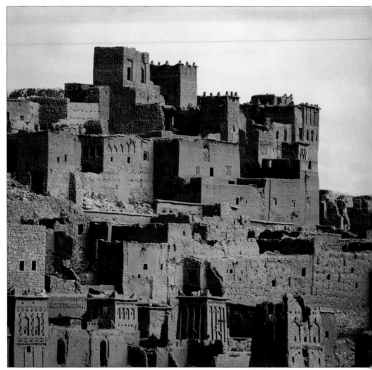

▼ **BELOW** This image of an old Moroccan town is striking for the uniform brown colour of the buildings, which encourages the viewer to focus on their shape and pattern.

▲ **ABOVE** The bold colours of the nets and the barrels on the fishing boat appear even stronger as they sit next to the neutral tones of the boat itself and the dark water.

▶ **RIGHT** An incredibly simple image that would lose all its drama if it wasn't for the highly saturated colours and perfectly placed vapour trail.

▼ **BELOW** With lots of tones of the same colour, low-contrast colour shots like these abstract petals have a calming and soothing effect.

Low-key Photography

Low-key images are those that comprise large areas of dark midtones and shadows. For this reason, such images are often perceived as sombre, moody and even threatening, and indeed most low-key images are exactly that. However, successful low-key images will often feature areas of bright highlights, which, as well as offering a visual balance to the mass of dark tones, can also inject an uplifting note into the image.

Many people when confronted with an overcast, cloudy day or a grey flat interior, will put their camera away and wait for the sun to come out. However, these occasions can often provide just the sort of light required for an effective low-key photograph – and, in fact, conditions just before or just after a storm are often the best time to capture a really dramatic landscape. Look for a break in the clouds, try to establish when the sun is likely to make a brief appearance and position yourself so that you have a suitable backdrop against which you can capture the sun's rays.

Expose for highlights

Remember in such conditions, and in fact in any low-key image where the small highlight areas are very bright, it's essential that you correctly expose for these areas. They are likely to become the focal point of the image, and it's better for the surrounding areas to be underexposed than for the highlights to be overexposed, or 'blown out'. This may be unavoidable if you're actually pointing the camera toward the sun or any other very bright region or object, for example, but such areas should be restricted to

Dynamic range

Often, particularly when shooting landscapes, the camera's sensor is unable to capture detail in both highlight and shadow regions. Use a tripod to overcome this, thus ensuring images have as wide a dynamic range as possible, with highlights and shadows containing visible detail. First expose for the highlights, then adjust the exposure for the shadow areas and take another shot. The two images can later be merged with editing software, resulting in a single image with high dynamic range.

▼ **BELOW** A classic low-key image; the dark, brooding sky and dark silhouetted landscape are uplifted by the sun's rays.

as small an area as possible. Use the LCD preview screen on the back of your camera and also take a look at the histogram (see pages 40–41) after each shot to make sure that the highlights are correctly exposed. Your camera may also feature a 'blown highlights' warning option, which will indicate overexposed areas on the LCD preview image through the use of a flashing colour.

Image editing

Once you have some candidates for potentially striking low-key images that include some interesting high-lights, open them on the computer and begin by cropping any excess dark background or foreground areas. You can then experiment with your imaging software's brightness controls to add even greater contrast and impact to the image.

Black and white

Since the vast majority of low-key images comprise expansive areas of dark and shadow tones interspersed with a few areas of bright highlights, such images lend themselves particularly well to black and white photography.

▲ **ABOVE** Even mundane items, such as these kitchen utensils, can make effective low-key subjects.

◄ **LEFT** The dark harbour walls and mud are offset by the white rowing boat in this low-key image.

▲ **ABOVE** Here the dark flag stones are nicely juxtaposed with the woodwork and light columns.

◄ **LEFT** Low-key effects can create sombre portraits, but here the Halloween costume sets the scene.

High-key Photography

In the way that successful low-key images rely on large areas of dark midtones and shadows juxtaposed with small areas of bright highlights, successful high-key photographs utilize expansive areas of white and light tones in which are found small regions of dark tones, or even black. Although not essential from a purist's point of view, these regions can often form the focal point of the image, so it's important that exposure is set to ensure that as much detail as possible is captured there.

High-key landscapes need to have a prevailing area of light tones and, for this reason, snowscapes, seascapes and large sand-dunes are ideal subject matter.

In terms of weather conditions, a dark, stormy sky full of forbidding clouds is unlikely to provide you with the ideal lighting conditions for high-key landscapes, but, at the same time, a clear, blue, cloud-free sky isn't entirely necessary either.

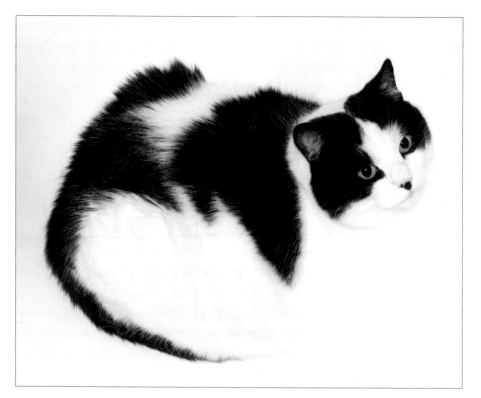

▼ **BELOW** High-key portraits result in a loss of skin texture and will often flatten facial features. Here the girl's face is framed by the darker hair, and the dark eyes make a strong focal point of the image.

▲ **ABOVE** This image was shot against a white background and deliberately overexposed. The white fur of the cat merges into the background, helping to emphasize the cat's monochromatic coloration.

Overexposure

The metering system in most digital cameras will always attempt to expose for a neutral grey. In other words, when faced with a potential high-key scene, the camera will automatically attempt to underexpose, in order to hold detail in the highlight areas.

You can set the camera's exposure compensation (EV) control to +1 or +2 to overcome this. It's quite probable that you'll get a 'blown highlight' warning if you review the image on the camera's LCD screen, but ignore this, as overexposed highlights are part of the artistic effect in high-key images.

Ideally, you'll want either hazy summer skies or misty, thin layers of cloud – as is often found during the late autumn and early winter months in temperate regions.

Expose for dark areas

Just as you should expose for highlights in low-key images, the opposite is true for high-key images. If you expose for the dark, shadowy areas, you'll capture any detail there – which is likely to be the focal point of the image – while it's less important to retain detail in the lighter areas. Most high-key images work best if little or no detail is visible in these lighter areas, as this helps to evoke and reinforce the light, delicate and airy nature of high-key images.

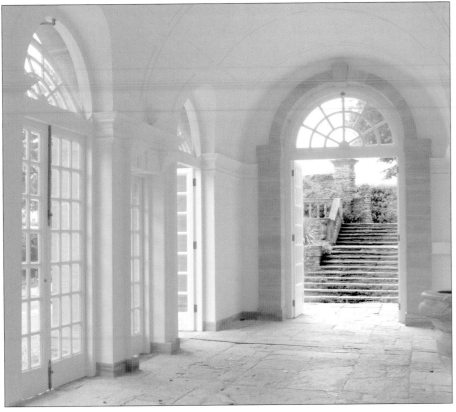

LEFT If you left the camera's metering system to its own devices with an interior shot like this, it would most likely underexpose, so the white walls came out a darker grey.

BELOW LEFT Setting the exposure to 1–2 stops more than the camera suggests (effectively overexposing the image) will help keep highlight areas light.

BELOW RIGHT Shadows that are dark, but not necessarily black, typify high-key images and give this style of photograph a light, airy feel.

BOTTOM An extreme example of a high-key picture, with very little highlight detail, and very few black tones.

Image editing

As with low-key pictures, once you have some candidates that you think would make great high-key images, open the photographs on your computer and begin experimenting. Start by cropping any excess background or foreground areas. You can then experiment with your imaging software's brightness controls to add even greater contrast and impact to the image.

Composing with Colour

Colour is an amazingly emotive and evocative subject. People will react to it whether they're aware of it or not, so for this reason, it must be considered with care in photography. Volumes have been written about how colour affects our emotions, and we can only touch on it briefly here. Much of it we inherently know. We all perceive red to be a passionate, powerful colour, for example, and a warning sign in both nature and the human environment. However, it is also a warm colour, of course – the colour of sunsets.

Red is generally considered the most 'advancing' colour in that it's often perceived as being closer than it really is, and therefore more likely to attract our attention. **Blue** is one of the most 'receding' colours in that it's often perceived as being more distant than it really is. Blue is a cool colour that evokes a sense of calm and peace in an image and it also provides a great contrast with red. **Green** is associated with nature, which is perhaps why it is often used to symbolize renewal and hope. It shares the same neighbourhood on the colour wheel as blue and is another receding colour that contrasts

▼ **BELOW** Brightly coloured, man-made objects are often great for bold abstract images, such as this swimming pool shot.

▲ **ABOVE** At sunrise and sunset the colour of light changes toward red, which gives landscape photographs a warm feel. This can be enhanced through the use of coloured filters, as demonstrated here.

with red. **Yellow** is more akin to red in that it is an advancing colour and one that helps to add warmth; it is the colour associated with the hot midday sun and fire.

These four colours are the most important in the visible spectrum. From these we get not only the additive primary colours (red, green, blue) of television sets, computer screens and digital cameras, but in terms of light, these colours mixed together to provide the secondary colours cyan, magenta and yellow. Also from our initial four colours we get the primary colours of the artist's paint palette (red, blue and yellow), from which we get the secondary colours violet, orange and green.

Saturated versus muted

Surprisingly, while vibrant, saturated colours have an initial impact and are good at attracting our attention – hence their liberal use in advertising, packaging and warning road signs – it's the muted colours that usually leave a longer-lasting impression in art and photography, particularly in landscapes and portraits. Unsaturated colours are more evocative and thought provoking, and the colours won't detract from the subject of the picture. However, if you're using colour to emphasize contrast, then they should be as vibrant as possible. Colours are most saturated in the

▶ **RIGHT** Although bright, saturated colours grab our attention initially, it is often muted and gentler colours that have a longer-lasting impact.

middle of a clear sunny day, when there are fewer shadows to interfere with expanses of colour. However, the cooler colour temperature at the end of the day can make reds, yellows and oranges more vibrant.

Desaturation

You can desaturate strong colour by using a long focal length under soft lighting conditions, as over long distances the light is more likely to be diffused by particles in the air. However, if you're using a long focal length lens or zoom setting, you may not get the framing that you want. Alternatively, you can also tone down the colour on your computer using your image software's colour controls.

▶ **RIGHT** Colour is the key to this simple yet striking landscape photograph. The richly saturated greens of the grass and blue of the sky are incredibly eye-catching.

◀ **LEFT** Less saturated colours, such as those found in some flowers, might not jump out of the page, but the effect is less jarring and far more calming.

▼ **BELOW** The powerful flavour of chillies is successfully evoked by the rich, saturated reds (which contrast well with the green stalks) in this image.

Lighting

The significance of lighting in photography cannot be overestimated – in fact the very word photography is derived from the Greek, literally meaning 'drawing or writing (*graphis*) with light (*photos*)'.

The strength, angle, temperature and quality of light – the last of which is affected by time of day, time of year, location and countless atmospheric conditions – will affect just about every aspect of an image. They will determine how bright the colours will be rendered, how strong and long the shadows will be, how visible distant objects are, and how much detail is obvious in foreground objects.

◀ **LEFT** Despite being shot in the shade, the bright red flowers contrast with the pale-coloured walls and green leaves, while the shadows in the background add to the sense of warmth.

▲▼ **ABOVE AND BELOW** These two images show the sea in very different light. The one below is dark and brooding and the lack of sun has created an almost monochromatic image, while the other, shot in strong late-afternoon sun, has saturated colours, strong shadows and a clear sky resulting in clear water.

Certain types of lighting can make objects appear flat or uniform in tone, while other lighting can make the same objects appear highly textured, pitted or undulating, and full of contrasting tones. In fact, the only parts of an image in which light does not carry as much significance is the subject, and the juxtaposition of the image's various elements to one another. In many ways, this is the very essence of photography. Setting aside studio photography, as a photographer it's essential that you are aware of the possibilities (and limitations) of different lighting situations.

Almost all of us, when we first become interested in photography, fall into the trap of assuming that you need bright sunny weather to create successful images. While it is true that these conditions do make for glorious photographs, so too can grey, overcast days – they're likely to elicit entirely different emotions in the viewer, but both conditions have the ability to produce striking images. As far as photography goes, there's no such thing as bad light. There may be inappropriate light for a specific shot, but in photography, 'bad' light should never stop play.

Timing

One of the most important traits all photographers should have, or need to develop, is patience. There will be many times when you know that the quality of the light is perfect for the scene in front of you, but you need some rays of light to highlight a specific element. It pays dividends to wait, as it could be the difference between a good photograph and an excellent one.

BELOW Early morning light enhances the soft misty atmosphere and brings a rosy glow to this shot of the River Thames, London.

Quality of Light

You will no doubt have heard or read about photographers discussing the 'quality' of light. While on a general level the term is used to describe anything from light temperature (such as the warm, red colour cast of a sunset), through to brightness levels, and the angle at which light is striking objects, more specifically, 'quality of light' strictly refers to how 'hard' or 'soft' it is.

Soft lighting

As its name suggests, soft lighting is a gentle, diffuse illumination and, outdoors, is usually the result of a layer of cloud. The water droplets and particles in the cloud scatter the sun's light rays as they pass through the cloud, sending the light in different directions. The most characteristic aspect of soft lighting is the lack of strong shadows, or sometimes any shadows at all. However, clouds come in an infinite variety of types, and different layers of cloud can often be moving at different speeds in relation to one another. For these reasons, the soft light of cloudy conditions can vary slightly from minute to minute.

In particular, with thick cloud conditions, when even the position of the sun in the sky is not discernible, objects can appear flat and free of texture, and colours somewhat muted. But that does not mean that such light cannot serve a useful photographic purpose. The lack of strong shadows and bright highlights can render complex shapes and scenes in a more intelligible fashion. Portraits are also sometimes more pleasing when there are no shadows to distort and alter peoples' features.

Hard lighting

Lighting is at its hardest when there's no cloud or haze to diffuse it – on clear summer days, for example. In these conditions the visibility tends to be good, making hard light ideal for 'long-view' landscapes. As we know from looking at texture, hard lighting can turn an apparently flat, featureless object into a mass of minute peaks and troughs. This is due to the strong shadows cast by direct, undiffused light. While this is often desirable and can be used to the photographer's advantage to create crisp, high-contrasting and dramatic images, deep shadows also have their drawbacks. They can render a busy scene, such as a shot of a market or street, too complex to view clearly because of the number of shadows, and they rarely help in portraits either.

▷ **RIGHT** To make your subject stand out from its surroundings, try taking the shot when the light on the background is soft.

▽ **BELOW** Soft, even lighting has ensured that the colours of the holly and berries are captured accurately, while the lack of strong shadows doesn't create a confusing image.

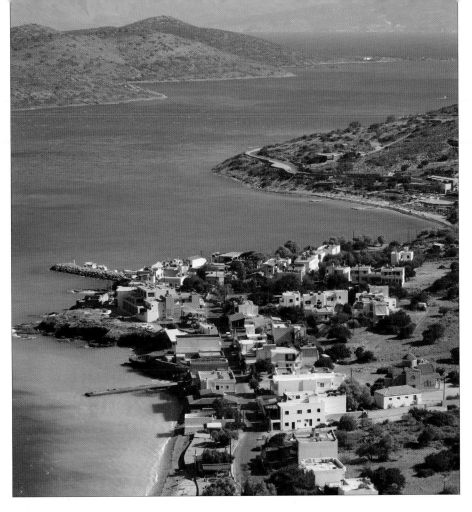

LEFT Hard lighting offers good visibility and crisp, clear photographs with sharply defined shadows.

SOFT AND HARD

Whether you shoot in soft, diffused light or strong, direct light has a significant impact on a photograph's appearance. Hard light will increase the contrast and colour saturation, while diffused light makes colours softer and also reduces the contrast for a more 'natural' appearance.

Soft light

Angle of light

One crucial aspect of hard light that must be considered is its angle and direction in relation to the subject or scene. The general characteristics and colours of an object lit from the front can look entirely different if lit from the side or from the back. So, having assessed the generic qualities of hard light, let's now look in more detail at how these qualities can alter the way in which individual objects or indeed entire scenes appear, depending on the direction of the light.

BELOW Strong, direct light is rarely flattering for portraits, but here the hat diffuses the light, so the face is softly lit.

Hard light

Direction of Light: Front and Side Lighting

With heavily diffused light, the position of the light source – which in most cases is likely to be the sun – is of little consequence in relation to the position of the subject. With hard light, however, the direction from which the subject is lit is fundamental to how it will appear in a photograph. How high or low the sun is in the sky also plays a significant role.

Frontal lighting

When the sun is located behind the photographer and falls directly onto the subject, the subject is said to be 'front lit'. This is perhaps the most common way to capture photographs and even those of us not that familiar with photography will probably remember being told that we should always shoot with the sun behind us.

Frontal lighting certainly has its benefits. With the sun directly behind us, shadows are cast away from the camera and, depending on the viewpoint, may well be out of our line of sight. Without strong shadows to cater for, getting an appropriate exposure for both light and dark areas is more straightforward with front-lit scenes due to the lack of contrast (or

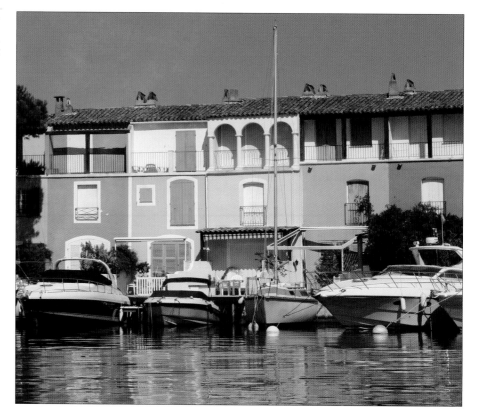

ABOVE Lit from the front, these houses appear almost two-dimensional, so the shot is about their flat colour, rather than form.

BELOW This partially buried wooden fence has been shot with side lighting, creating shadows that make for a pleasing, almost abstract effect. The side lighting also helps to bring out the texture in the sand.

low dynamic range). The photograph's colours also tend to be more evenly illuminated, so subtleties in tone become increasingly apparent.

The drawback of frontal lighting is that the lack of shadows will underplay the visibility of any texture the subject might have, and potentially reduce perspective across the entire scene. For these reasons shots may appear rather flat and lacking in any depth.

For really successful frontally lit images, you should be relying on interesting and strong colour and tonal contrast. Bear in mind, too, that reflective surfaces will throw back most light when front lit. Finally, do be mindful of your own shadow when shooting with the sun behind you. Depending on how low it is in the sky, the sun could cast your shadow a surprisingly long way into the scene you're photographing and potentially ruin a great shot. Some photographers, if confronted with this problem, will

▶ **RIGHT** The light coming from the side helps describe the form of the towers' unusually shaped roofs. If the light was coming from the front they would lose their form.

try to disguise their body shape so that it resembles less a human figure and more an anonymous shrub, or whatever is appropriate for the scene.

Side lighting

With the sun to one side of both you and the subject, the image is said to be side lit. While front lighting tends to flatten objects, side lighting emphasizes texture and form as shadows are prominent and potentially long, depending on how low the sun is.

Side lighting also adds drama to an image. Parts of a scene may be well lit and the colours saturated, while other parts may be in shadow and their colours muted. In very bright, side-lit situations, the scene may be so heavily contrasting, with bright, white high-

lights and dark, almost black shadows (creating a very high dynamic range), that the camera's sensor won't be able to capture all the detail in the scene. In these situations you must decide to expose either for the shadows or the highlights. The decision will ultimately be down to the subject matter and the emotions you are trying to evoke in the viewer. For these reasons, it's sensible to bracket high-contrast, side-lit scenes, as that way you'll have a greater chance of getting an exposure that works. You can further increase your chances of success by shooting RAW (see page 17).

▼ **BELOW** Strong side lighting creates bright highlights and deep shadows, which gives a greater idea of the subject's form.

▼ **BELOW LEFT** Shooting group shots in bright sunshine has many pitfalls. To avoid subjects squinting into the sun and strong shadows running down their faces, try positioning the group so that they're lit from the side.

Front versus side

• Front lighting reduces the texture of a subject, but can help make strong colours appear even bolder.

• Lighting coming from the side will reveal a subject's form, but watch out for confusing shadows.

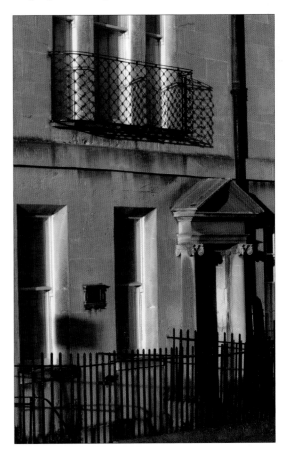

Direction of Light: Back Lighting

Another popular way of working with direct, undiffused light is to place the subject more or less between the sun and the camera. This is known as back lighting a subject, and the technique is sometimes referred to as *contre jour*, French for 'against the day'. Back lighting can create dramatic results due to the high contrast inherent in back-lit scenes.

Silhouettes

The best-known back-lit technique is the silhouette. To shoot a silhouette, simply position the subject directly in front of a large bright area, or indeed the sun itself, and the camera will usually automatically underexpose the subject to create the silhouette. Ensuring that the sun is masked by the subject usually works best, otherwise you run the risk of not being able to capture any information at all due to the brightness of the sun. Unless the subject is translucent you're unlikely to capture any detail, colour or texture. The only clue as to what the subject is will be its outline shape. Silhouettes can, of course, make for very powerful images, but it's important to choose your subject on the merits of its shape alone and to position it so its shape is shown to best advantage. The most striking silhouettes have an almost uniform, light-coloured background to make the subject most obvious.

Buildings (particularly structures with interesting shapes such as bridges or piers), trees, a face in profile – in fact anything, as long as it has an interesting or emotive shape – make excellent subjects for a silhouette.

Translucency

For variation, try shooting a translucent object placed in front of the light source. Depending on the object, fine detail will be visible, such as the veins of a leaf, and colours will be bright and saturated. You do need to be careful, however, not to overexpose the subject.

Rim lighting

As dramatic as silhouettes are, the effect should be used sparingly in any portfolio. There are other back-lighting effects that are just as striking. Rim lighting is a form of back lighting in which the light source is behind, but also slightly off to one side. The resulting shot, depending on the object being photographed and the background, will have brightly lit, almost glowing edges, and can make for a spectacular image.

BELOW Shooting directly into a light source increases the risk of 'lens flare' in your picture. Here, it is shown by the purple and green patches of colour in the corners.

RIGHT Back lighting can be used effectively to throw long shadows toward the camera creating a dramatic result.

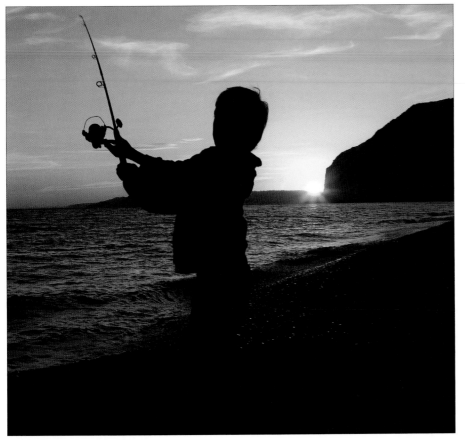

BELOW Not all portraits need to be lit from the front so we can see every detail in the subject. Lighting from behind can create equally attractive photographs.

ABOVE The most striking silhouettes are made when you have a subject that is recognizable, even when there is no detail – as in this shot of a boy fishing.

BELOW Rim lighting produces very striking results, with the heavy lighting from behind and to the side of the subjects, creating glowing highlights.

Flare

Lens flare is apparent in silhouettes or other forms of back-lit shots in the form of rows of hexagonal-shaped circles of light emanating from the sun (or any other light source). The shape of the light pools is determined by the shape of the lens' aperture (or diaphragm) when the shot is taken. Although this type of lens flare (which is caused by reflections within the camera's lens) can add atmosphere to a shot, it is better to try to prevent it. This is why you sometimes see a lens fitted with a lens hood, which is a petal- or cup-shaped piece of plastic that fits on the end of the lens and acts as a sunshade for the lens.

Taking back-lit shots

- Silhouettes work best when you can identify the subject only by the shape of its outline.
- Use light from behind and to the side of the subject for intense highlights and added drama.
- Avoid lens flare by shielding the front of the lens from the light by using a lens hood.
- Remember that colour will usually be very muted with most back-lit shots; if colour is an important element of the shot, try front lighting.

Available Light

In photography 'available light' refers to any natural light source used to light a scene, and while this includes daylight for outdoor photography, here we're going to concentrate on daylight (and standard domestic lighting) for indoor photography and certain natural sources for night-time.

Although some keen amateur photographers may own a small lighting set-up, many will not, so all photographers will have to rely on available, or 'existing' light, such as standard tungsten light bulbs, at some point, especially when taking photographs indoors or outdoors during late evening or at night.

Of course just about every camera today has a small flash built into the body of the camera (and later we'll be looking in more detail at what we should expect from built-in flash units), but as useful as they are, such units usually only provide relatively low light levels and often subjects are harshly lit.

Indoors

Using available indoor light, by which we mean daylight from windows shining into a room and normal domestic lighting, can result in very pleasing images. Pictures taken using available light are often much more atmospheric and exhibit a greater sense of realism than those that have been painstakingly lit using a variety of studio lights and accessories.

The most important aspect to bear in mind when taking photographs under such lighting conditions is that, when captured, images will appear to have far more pronounced areas of light and shade than seemed apparent to the naked eye. When we spend time in a room our eyes are constantly and almost instantaneously

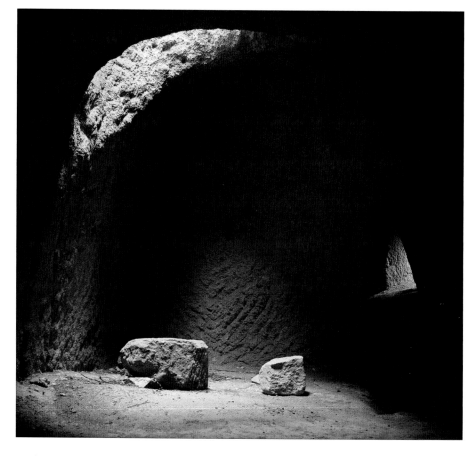

▼ **BELOW** Simple side lighting from a window was used in this pet portrait.

▲ **ABOVE** Using the available light from the two 'windows' in this cave, the rocks on the floor have been picked out and appear to be incredibly three dimensional.

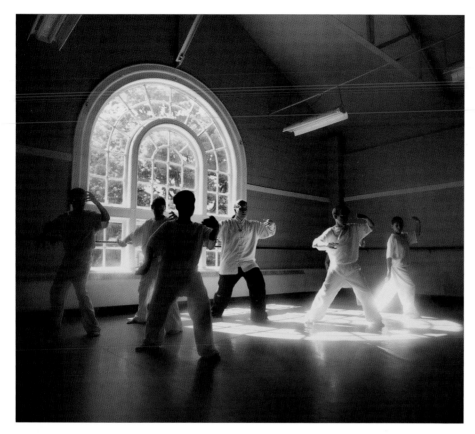

LEFT Using solely the light entering from the arched window has resulted in a highly atmospheric photograph.

Using natural light

- Ambient light will allow you to retain more of the atmosphere of a scene than flash will.
- Use slow shutter speeds, wide apertures or high ISO settings in low-light conditions.
- Remember, however, that high ISO settings will introduce digital noise.

ABOVE Here the light from a window not only illuminates the image on the wall, it also becomes part of the picture.

BELOW Using the light from the fire has kept all the atmosphere of this scene. Flash would have ruined the shot in an instant.

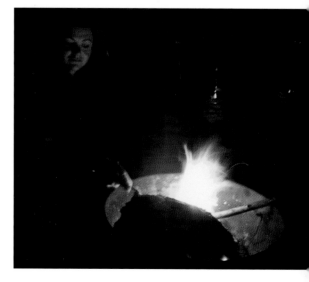

adjusting for the well-lit and dimly lit areas as we look around, which create the appearance of a fairly evenly lit room. However, the camera is only capturing one specific part of the room at one specific moment, so resulting images will appear to have greater contrast. Use this to your advantage to place emphasis on certain elements or people – for example, sit someone in a chair that has been positioned in a brighter area of a room and you'll notice that the darker regions of the room will recede, placing greater emphasis on the sitter.

Setting exposure

If you're including a window in the shot, the comparative brightness of the window in relation to the rest of the room needs to be accounted for when setting exposure. Take a reading from a bright region near to the window, press the exposure lock button, recompose the shot and take the picture. Depending on the strength of the light coming through the window, you should be able to hold most of the detail in the room without 'burning out' too much of the window

itself. Try bracketing the exposure if you're uncertain and checking the results on the camera's LCD screen.

Colour cast

Given the relatively low temperature of tungsten light bulbs – the most commonly used bulbs in the home – make sure that the camera's white balance setting is set to Tungsten or Auto to counteract the orange colour cast caused by such lighting. Even then, you may find that images will suffer from a colour cast that you'll have to correct using editing software.

Tripod versus ISO

With low-light conditions there's a risk of camera shake if the shutter speed is insufficiently fast. If you don't have a tripod, increase the ISO setting, but do this in stages as noise from high ISO settings is more apparent in dark scenes (see pages 14–15). If you do have a tripod, then you can shoot at the lowest possible ISO setting without the risk of camera shake. Bear in mind that even relatively slow-moving action may blur at speeds of $^{1}/_{15}$ sec or longer.

Shadows

Any discussion about the significance of light in photography would not be complete without turning our thoughts to shadows. In many ways, shadows help to reinforce the prevailing lighting conditions and add atmosphere to an image. We recognize the presence of bright sunlight in an image not just by bright highlights or saturated colours, but also by deep black shadows. Equally, the lack of strong shadow will lower the overall contrast of an image and give a softer look to a picture.

Almost all photographs that are taken outdoors during daylight hours will contain shadows, except for those taken under the most diffused lighting conditions. However, shadows are very easy to overlook when composing an image, as we tend to focus our attention on the subject of a shot. Also, because shadows are such a common phenomenon they don't register – until we review the shots and discover that strong shadows have spoiled the composition.

▲ **ABOVE** Without the shadows in this wintry scene the snow would be a flat, featureless expanse of white.

▼ **BELOW** The Grand Canyon with the sun low in the sky is modelled by the shadows, which help to reinforce the Canyon's peaks and troughs and add scale and perspective.

Strong light

When taking photographs outdoors, it is worth deliberately looking for the shadows in a potential scene. Check to see if your position in relation to the sun results in any shadows falling across an important compositional element of the photograph. Although altering your position won't change the direction in which the shadows are cast, you may discover that an alternative angle provides a similar shot that makes the shadow invisible, or less of a distraction.

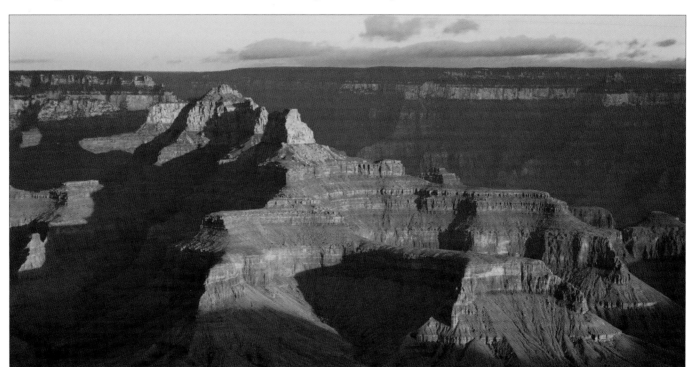

Composition

An alternative to eliminating shadows from an image is to look deliberately for ways in which to include them. Not only can they add to the image by introducing their own unique, obscure shapes, but they can also help to draw the viewer into an image – often a shadow can act as a leading line taking the viewer directly to the subject of the photograph.

Shadows can also provide visual clues about an image – such as the time of day the photograph was taken, how bright (or overcast) the conditions were and even the type of environment in which the image was shot. While it may be obvious from the subject of the picture itself whether the image was taken in a city or in a forest, shadows cast by objects not visible in the scene will help to evoke the atmosphere, whether they're the geometric, blocky shadows of buildings or the organic shapes of branches or leaf fronds.

Form and texture

With light coming in at a low, raking angle, shadows can also help to tease out the texture from objects and to emphasize their form. This modelling attribute can be used in a variety of photographic genres – from nudes to landscapes – whenever you want to reveal the texture of your subject.

▲ **ABOVE** Although taken on a sunny day, the cool shadows contrast pleasantly with the pale yellow sand.

▶ **RIGHT** Low-angle light casts shadows that help describe a subject's form.

▼ **BELOW** In this woodland scene, the long shadows add another layer to the image, making it all the more dramatic.

Low-light and Night Photography

If captured well, low-light and night scenes can result in wonderfully strong, atmospheric shots. Quite understandably, people are often put off capturing low-light or night-time shots thinking that the lack of light throws up too many technical difficulties to overcome. However, with a little perseverance and a certain amount of trial and error, the skills of low-light photography can be quickly mastered.

Just about any scene is suitable for low-light treatment – especially cityscapes. With their numerous and variously coloured lights and towering skylines, cityscapes usually provide the most dramatic night images, while rural scenes often work best just after the sun has set rather than late at night. As a rule of thumb, when taking photographs of low-light landscapes, there will still be sufficient light available to capture a photograph that will adequately show the surrounding countryside up to around 30 minutes after the sun has set, or less in the Tropics.

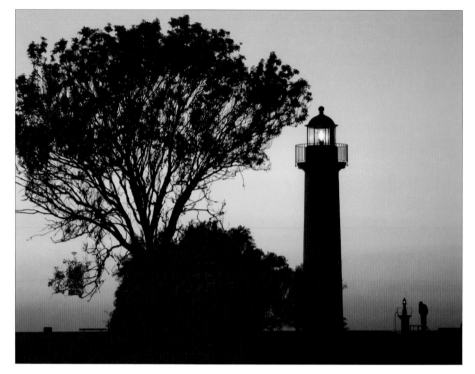

Noise

A recurring issue with low-light photography is digital noise and, depending on your camera, it may well always be present in night shots. However, there are actions you can take to keep noise to a minimum. The most obvious is to use as low an ISO setting

ABOVE A sunset on a clear summer's day is a good time for photographs of silhouettes. Here, the light of the lighthouse is a focal point.

BELOW Cities at 'night' can create colourful and evocative images. The best time to capture city lights is at twilight, about 45 minutes after the sun has set, rather than at night.

as possible. This means that you'll need a tripod or a makeshift surface on which to rest the camera while taking the shot. If there is a noise-reduction facility available on your camera, try using this. It will double the time it takes for the images to be saved, but may help reduce background noise.

White balance

With long exposures, there is a chance that the auto white balance setting (which neutralizes colour casts created by certain temperatures of light) will be tricked by the various light sources, especially in cityscapes where light sources may include car head-lights, neon signs, streetlamps and so on. The variety of light sources and resulting colour casts can often create a pleasing result.

However, if you want white objects to appear white, you need to manually set the white balance. Most advanced cameras allow you to do this with a 'custom white balance' setting. With the camera set to 'custom white balance' (the setting name may vary depending on the manufacturer), fill the frame and photograph a white object that you wish to be reproduced as white. The camera will automatically allow for the overall colour temperature and white objects will appear white.

▲ **ABOVE** At sunrise and sunset the sky can turn from a rich blue to a deep orange-red in an instant, but choosing the right white balance is crucial.

▶ **RIGHT** This shot almost looks like a toned black-and-white picture, with its matching sky and water. Only the distant yellow light tells you it isn't.

▼ **BELOW** Towns and cities at night make for good low-light subjects thanks to the mix of colour temperatures in the lighting – from 'white' to orange.

Low-light composition

Stunning results can be achieved in low-light conditions and it certainly pays to experiment with different sources of light, whether it's the warm glow of a sunset or the artificial lighting from office blocks or street lighting.

Look out for reflective surfaces, such as ponds, lakes or even wet pavements. The reflected light will not only give you more illumination to experiment with, but the reflected image can add another dimension to your composition.

Using Flash

At one time or another, all of us need a relatively powerful, if short-lived, light source that enables us to take photographs at night or indoors, using shutter speeds that are fast enough to freeze action. For that reason most digital cameras, from point and shoot to dSLRs, come equipped with a built-in flash.

Built-in flash

As useful as built-in flash is – and it certainly makes it possible to shoot in some situations where, without it, you may not have any usable images at all – such units do have limitations.

The first drawback is the effective range, as most on-camera flashes are only capable of throwing light a distance of between 5ft (1.5m) and 10ft (3m) from the camera, which won't be powerful enough to light larger groups or scenes.

The other significant problem is 'redeye'. This occurs because the flash unit is so close to the axis of the lens. When the flash fires, it fires directly into the subject's eyes, bounces off the retina in the back of the eye, and

flash head

LCD infomation panel

test firing button/ ready light

autofocus assist light

locking ring

set button/exposure controls

▲ **ABOVE** External flash units, such as this Canon model, provide more powerful lighting and a much greater degree of control than on-camera flash units.

illuminates the eye's blood vessels. The proximity of the flash to the lens can also be a problem with wide-angle lenses on dSLRs, as the flash isn't designed to cover the width of a scene visible through a wide-angle lens. The result is a vignetted image, in

which the corners appear darker than the central part of the image. Finally, perhaps the worst problem of all with built-in flash is simply the quality of light it produces. Built-in flash will often produce stark pictures with harsh shadows. While this can be partly remedied by reducing the strength of the flash using the camera's 'flash exposure compensation' setting (if it has one), you may find that large parts of the image are underexposed.

▲ **ABOVE** These two shots of an arched corridor show how flash can only throw light a certain distance. The image on the left was taken using a tripod and long exposure; the daylight entering from the right has provided a more or less evenly lit corridor. The one on the right was taken with flash, and clearly shows the arches becoming progressively darker the farther they are from the flash.

▲ **ABOVE** Flash units are a convenient way of lighting a subject when there is insufficient ambient light available. However, getting natural looking light can be problematic.

LEFT You don't just need to think of flash as a low-light tool. Here (in the picture on the right), it's been used in strong sunlight to fill-in the shadows on the subject's face.

Fill-in flash

Despite these drawbacks, built-in flash is an excellent tool for 'fill-in' lighting. It may seem strange to use flash during the day, but you'll probably have noticed that whenever you see wedding photographers or photo-journalists in action, they'll invariably have a flashgun attached to their cameras, even if the weather is bright and sunny. This is used for fill-in flash.

Fill-in flash throws additional light onto a subject that may be in shadow or underexposed due to strong back lighting. In both cases using flash will improve the quality of the images, adding brightness and colour to an otherwise drab element of the image. Because fill-in flash doesn't need to be particularly powerful, a camera's built-in flash is often ideal for the job.

Flashguns

If you find that you're increasingly relying on the camera's built-in flash and you're not happy with the results, you may want to consider buying a flashgun. These are self-powered flash units that are fixed to the top of the camera via the camera's 'hot shoe' plate. Flashguns vary enormously in price depending on how powerful they are and how sophisticated the metering system, but for a relatively modest outlay you can improve the quality of your flash photography enormously using such a device.

Most of today's flashguns can be set to synchronize automatically with the camera so that the shutter opens at the same time the flash fires, as it does with the built-in flash. Often a 'pre-flash' is fired so that the camera's metering system can set the correct exposure for the subject (known as Through The Lens, or TTL, flash). Sophisticated flashguns will also take information from the camera's focusing system to gauge the distance from camera to subject, and therefore determine more precisely how much light is needed for an accurate exposure.

Power and bounce

The greatest benefit of using a flashgun is that it produces more light than a built-in flash. One obvious advantage of this is that more distant objects can be lit, but there's another, more significant benefit. The most useful flashguns have heads that tilt (and swivel), allowing you to 'bounce' the light off walls, ceilings or other reflective surfaces. Bounced flash produces much softer light, as in effect the light is coming from a much larger surface area, which has the effect of diffusing shadows. You need the increased power from a flashgun to make the most of this bounced flash effect. Additionally, because the light is not coming directly from the camera, but from above (or to the side), the lighting appears more natural. Finally, because the flash unit of a flashgun sits much higher than that of a built-in flash unit, there's a much reduced risk of redeye.

ABOVE When used direct from the camera, a flash creates hard shadows (top). Bouncing it off the ceiling will give a much more natural looking result (bottom).

Diffusers

Another way in which to soften light from a flashgun is to fit a diffuser. Diffusers are moulded pieces of white translucent plastic that fit over the head of the gun and spread the light when the flash fires. By their very nature, diffusers drastically cut down the range of the flashgun – another reason why professionals opt for the most powerful units – but they give a light that looks much softer and far more natural than direct flash.

When to Shoot

So many factors govern lighting that to make any hard and fast rules about the best time to take photographs would be meaningless – season, location and local weather conditions all affect the quality, strength, direction and colour of light.

The environment in which you live will offer varying photographic opportunities depending on the prevailing weather conditions. For example, a gentle mist and low-lying cloud may provide the perfect conditions for certain rural landscapes but they would do absolutely nothing for a city shot.

However, it's important to know what sort of results you can expect under certain lighting conditions, so you learn to know what type of photograph works best in the conditions you're shooting under. This, of course, can only come with experience, using your eyes and a certain amount of common sense.

Morning

Sunny mornings, and specifically within a hour of the sun rising above the horizon, will provide a low, raking

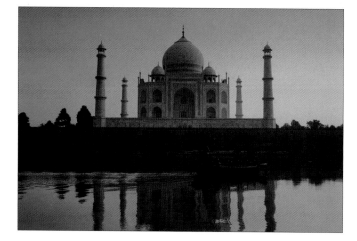

BELOW These two images of the Taj Mahal, although not taken from the same place, still show how the light at different times of the day can radically alter the same scene.

ABOVE Clear, late afternoons in temperate regions can often impart a warm, rosy glow to images. Make sure the camera's Auto white balance doesn't try to 'correct' the red glow resulting in a more neutral white colour.

light that offers the opportunity to shoot all four major variations of lighting – frontal, side, back and rim. This makes early morning one of the most dynamic times to be out with a camera. Depending on the season, you may also have early morning mist in low-lying areas or over standing water, and the sun will reflect strongly off tall buildings. At this time of day, the light temperature will be relatively low, creating a glowing orange cast, while the sun itself can make a spectacular subject.

Mid-morning can provide a good compromise between the first hour or so after sunrise and midday. There's variation in the direction of light, and shadows will be flattering, but the light is more neutral and colours will reproduce more accurately. Look for texture, modelling shadows and subtle, yet distinct, colour.

By midday, with the sun high in the sky, light is at its harshest and you need to turn your attention away from subtle modelling and flattering shadows and look for well-defined, interesting shapes, and bright, saturated colours. The consistent quality of light at this time of day tends to produce sharp, crisp images, but remember that strong shadows may add confusion to certain scenes.

LEFT Although early morning haze reduces visibility and distant detail, it's perfect for atmospheric landscape shots, especially when using a telephoto lens or zoom setting.

Some of the most dramatic shots can be taken just before or just after a storm. At such times it's not unusual to have a backdrop of black, forbidding skies while the foreground is bathed in strong sunlight. Furthermore, sooner or later, as the clouds disperse, the sun's rays will break cover and appear as powerful beams of light.

Hazy days

Haze can bring unique qualities of light to a variety of scenes. As well as diffusing harsh light and helping to soften shadows, haze can add a sense of depth by flattening and desaturating colour. This can result in an evocative layering effect if there are distant ranges of hills. To make the most of this effect, shoot with a telephoto setting or lens.

Mid-afternoon and sunsets

As with mid-morning and dawn, from mid-afternoon until about 30 minutes after the sun has set, the light temperature will decrease and take on an increasingly golden hue. Shadows will lengthen and light levels will gradually decrease. This is a good time to look for potential silhouette subjects, as a glowing red sun can make for a more interesting backdrop to a silhouette than a bright white mass. Even after the sun has set, keep taking shots, as successful low-light images during twilight can be among the most atmospheric, with the sun's afterglow helping to create soft and subtle tonal gradations.

Finally, consider indoor light shots available at this time of day. With the sun low in the sky, you may find that some parts of a room are lit with shafts of strong light, throwing other parts into shadow.

Cloudy days

The quality and strength of light on cloudy days will vary depending on the types of cloud and how numerous they are. Generally, cloud will soften light and help diffuse shadows. On windy, predominantly sunny days, scudding clouds create fluctuating levels of light, which require patience on the part of the photographer as he or she waits for the clouds to pass over and bathe the scene in sunlight. This is often a time when strong light and shade can be captured, adding tonal interest to a composition.

A vast blanket of cloud will have a dulling effect. Shadows will all but disappear, along with the chances of exploiting texture and form. However, such soft, consistent light can often simplify potentially complex scenes such as woods and forests, so use this light to exploit intricate shapes and subtle colour variations.

RIGHT Around 30 to 45 minutes after the sun has set (or less in the Tropics), is the best time to photograph buildings that are artificially lit. The light remains strong enough to show surrounding detail, but the building still appears well lit.

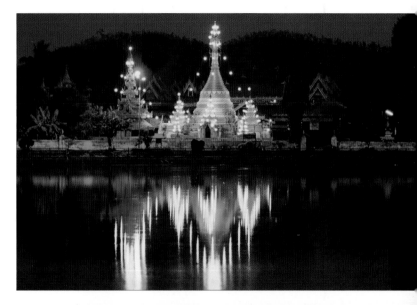

RIGHT Around midday, when the sun is high in the sky, light is at its most neutral colour, and if the sky is clear, this is when images will be at their sharpest.

Lighting – Try It Yourself

An effective way to discover the impact of different lighting conditions is to use a 'source' scene and shoot it at different times of the day, and preferably at different times of the year and under varying weather conditions.

For the sake of convenience, select a scene that is within easy reach; the more varied the scene the better. For example, try to find a location that includes natural objects such as fields, trees, rocks and grass, as well as artificial ones, such as buildings, roads or any other man-made structures. That way, you'll hopefully see how the changing quality of light impacts on a wide variety of surfaces, textures, shapes and forms.

Time of year

When the weather looks set to be predominantly sunny, aim to get to your location just before sunrise. Set up the shot with a focal length of around 50mm, using a tripod so you can shoot at the lowest ISO setting. Carefully make a note of the position you've taken up, and at sunrise take a few shots. Return to the same spot every hour, or if that's not possible, at least every two hours, and photograph the same scene. Keep returning to the location until sunset, at which point take your final shots.

Review

Download the photographs onto a computer and review them. The first thing you'll notice is the way in which the scene becomes increasingly well lit as the sun begins to rise. Depending on the scene, long shadows may form and, depending on the weather conditions, time of year and location, you'll see a gradual shift in colour temperature – from red to neutral – as the sun progresses across the sky.

By midday, shadows are more likely to have shortened, but they may well have strengthened, and any colour will appear more saturated. However, most noticeable will be the way in which objects are lit – whether it's side, front or back lighting. As the sun moves in the sky, surfaces will be lit in different ways and this will have the biggest impact on the image.

As noon passes and the sun begins its descent into the west, shadows will gradually start to grow longer, surfaces that were not previously lit may become illuminated, and colours will become more muted.

By late afternoon, the light will cast everything in a rosy glow (depending on time of year, location and weather conditions), while shadows will lengthen. As the sun sets, elements of the scene may be visible only in silhouette and any clouds will reflect the red glow of the setting sun.

Time of year

Try to repeat this exercise at various times of the year to see what impact the changing seasons have on your environment. Test whether you can tell the difference between the quality and temperature of the light on a sunny summer's day and a sunny winter one. When younger, those of us brought up in a mild temperate climate would often equate a blue sky with warm weather, but in fact it's impossible to tell the temperature from a blue sky alone.

▼ **BELOW** Each part of the day will bring its own unique quality of light and radically alter how a particular scene photographs.

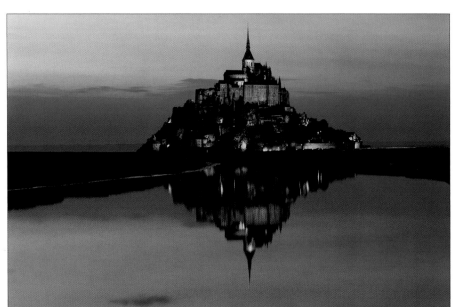

Weather conditions

Deliberately photograph your selected location in a variety of weather conditions. Test out if the old adage that dull weather makes for dull photographs is true in the case of your chosen scene. If so, then what weather conditions are needed to bring a bit of sparkle to the shot? Does it require a sunny day or can subtleties of light, shade and tone be teased out under overcast conditions?

06.30

07.30

09.30

12.00

14.00

16.00

18.00

THIS PAGE To see the effect that different lighting conditions have on a picture, find a suitable location and take a series of pictures throughout the day – from sunrise through to sunset. As morning changes to afternoon and then evening (left), so the shadows change size and direction, while the colour of the light is also constantly shifting from warm to cool colours.

Focal Length

A lens's focal length is the distance between its optical centre (the point at which the light rays begin to converge), and the focal plane (the surface of the image sensor). Focal length is always measured in millimeters (mm). In the days when the majority of keen amateurs and professionals used 35mm film cameras, understanding focal length was relatively straightforward. However, digital cameras – or more accurately the varying sensor sizes used in digital cameras – have made the issue of focal length less easy to understand.

Whereas all lenses were once designed to project an image onto the standard 35mm (24 x 36mm) film frame, because of the numerous different sensor sizes available in today's dSLR cameras, a lens of a specific focal length will project a different view of a scene, often increasing the effective focal length.

Equivalent focal length
Let's try to explain this more clearly using numbers. A 35mm film frame, or a 'full-frame' digital sensor, has a diagonal measurement of 43mm.

Therefore, to provide an unmagnified, standard view, a lens would need a focal length of 43mm (historically this has been rounded up to 50mm).

A number of popular compact zoom cameras have much smaller sensors, with a diagonal measurement of 9.5mm (the measurement of a standard 1/1.7-in sensor). With a sensor measuring 9.5mm, the lens only needs a focal length of 9.5mm to achieve a x1 magnification.

So, while a theoretical 43mm lens provides a standard view on a full-frame sensor (x1 magnification – 43 divided by 43 = 1), on a smaller sensor measuring 9.5mm diagonally, the magnification would be 43 divided by 9.5 = 4.53, or the equivalent focal length (efl) 43 x 4.53 = 195mm, which is quite a powerful telephoto lens.

On many compact zoom cameras you may see the lens labelled along the lines of 9–70mm, which would make no sense in the 35mm format, but when converted to allow for the smaller sensor size this lens provides the equivalent focal lengths (efl) of 9 x 4.53 = 41mm, zooming to 70 x 4.53 = 317mm.

To make sense of these potentially confusing focal lengths, the equivalent focal length is often used in conjunction with real focal lengths in magazines, websites and sales material to give people a point of reference. This is why many hybrid camera lenses are advertised as 38–380mm (or 10x) instead of, or as well as, their true focal lengths.

Angle of view

A lens's focal length determines its angle of view. The longer the focal length, the narrower the angle of view and the greater the degree of subject enlargement. The shorter the focal length, the wider the angle of view and the smaller the same subject appears. With hindsight, if lenses were described by their angle of view we wouldn't have the confusion over focal lengths. The diagram below shows the angles of view for the four main types of lens used by dSLRs – wide-angle, standard, telephoto and extreme telephoto.

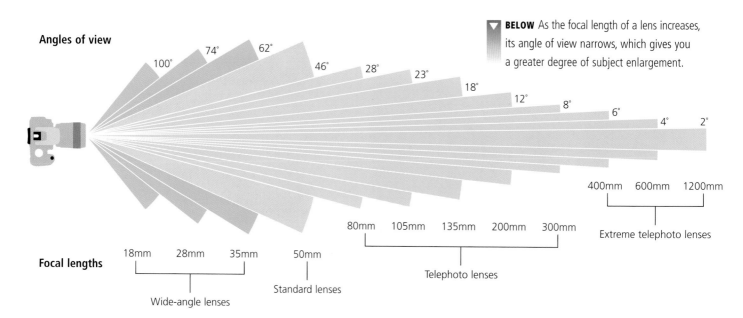

BELOW As the focal length of a lens increases, its angle of view narrows, which gives you a greater degree of subject enlargement.

| efl 16mm | efl 32mm | efl 56mm | efl 112mm |

| efl 160mm | efl 220mm | efl 320mm | efl 480mm |

ABOVE Focal lengths are measured in millimetres (mm) and range from effective wide-angle focal lengths of around 16mm (or less) to equivalent telephoto lengths of 480mm (or more).

APS

The vast majority of dSLRs use APS-sized sensors. APS (Advanced Photo System) was originally a film format developed for point-and-shoot cameras. The system is now almost defunct, but the format has been taken up by the major camera manufacturers as a popular sensor size for dSLRs, because it is less expensive to manufacture, while still providing excellent images. To confuse matters slightly more, there are a number of APS sizes, but most are around 22 x 15mm.

CROP FACTOR

APS sensors are smaller than full-frame 35mm sensors, and therefore experience the same issue with focal length measurements. To standardize things, interchangeable lenses for dSLRs are labelled with their actual focal length. DSLR owners need to know the size of the sensor in their particular camera to find the equivalent focal length. The same calculation (dividing the diagonals) is carried out, and the result is often expressed as the 'crop factor'. For example, Canon's semi-professional dSLRs use a sensor with a diagonal of close to 27mm, which gives a crop factor of 1.6.

This means that to find the efl for a lens attached to the body, the photographer multiplies the real focal length by 1.6 – so a 60mm lens has an efl of 95mm. Nikon, Fuji and Sony use sensors with a crop factor of 1.5, so a 60mm lens on these models has an efl of 90mm.

1.6 crop factor

Short Focal Length

Lenses with an equivalent focal length of between 18mm and 35mm are described as having a short focal length. Offering an angle of view of between 100° (efl 18mm) and 62° (efl 35mm), they are also known as wide-angle lenses as they provide an angle of view greater than that seen by human vision (around 46°).

A wide-angle lens's ability to capture such a wide angle of view has a number of benefits and can be used to great compositional effect. One of the most common uses of a wide-angle lens is photographing interiors. With such a wide-angle of view, these lenses can photograph much more of a room than a standard (efl 35–50mm) lens.

This ability to capture such wide views is also often used in landscape photography to help emphasize wide-open spaces, and create a sense of emptiness. As well as having the ability to encompass more of a scene, wide-angle lenses also tend to differentiate more clearly between the various planes within a scene,

clearly separating the foreground, middle-distance and background objects from each other.

Depth of field

One of the most useful optical properties of wide-angle lenses is their great depth of field, as the shorter the focal length, the greater the depth of field at the same aperture setting (see pages 82–83). This allows the

photographer to ensure that very close foreground objects are in focus, as well as distant objects. This can bring an increased illusion of depth to an image, but the disadvantage is that it becomes harder to selectively blur specific elements within a scene.

A wide-angle lens's short focal length is particularly helpful with hand-held photography, as the risk of camera shake is reduced the shorter the focal

▼ **BELOW** When you can't move too far back from your subject, use a wide-angle lens to squeeze in as much of the scene as possible.

▲ **ABOVE** Wide-angle lenses let you get a lot of a scene in the frame, and the increased depth of field also lets you get everything sharp.

▼ **BELOW** Short focal-length lenses can introduce a 'barrel distortion' effect, in which vertical lines, such as walls, seem to bulge outwards.

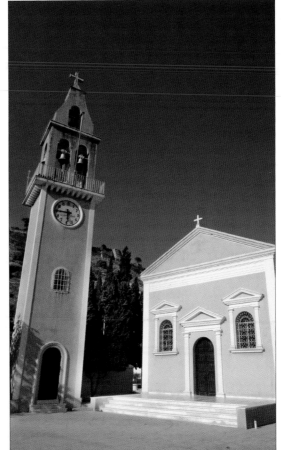

FAR LEFT Using a wide-angle lens indoors will help you get as much of the interior in the frame as possible, but there can be potential problems with distortion.

LEFT 'Converging verticals' can occur because of a wide-angle lens's angle of view.

length of the lens. For example, shooting at $^1/_{30}$ sec with a standard lens setting of between 35–50mm would often result in camera blur, but with an effective focal length of 18mm camera shake is much less likely.

Distortion

Another key characteristic of wide-angle lenses is distortion – again, the shorter the focal length the greater the distortion. This effect becomes most apparent in photographs that include objects with straight lines, such as buildings. One form of distortion, which is known as 'barrel' distortion, makes vertical and horizontal lines bulge outward, most noticeably at the edges of the frame. Wide-angle and particularly super wide-angle lenses are not appropriate for portraits due to the effect of barrel distortion, unless you're aiming for a deliberate effect.

Another issue associated with wide-angle lenses is converging verticals – a form of distortion in which lines appear to move closer together the higher they rise. This is most noticeable in architectural shots and is a result of the wide angle of view from a wide-angle lens.

True wide angle

For those owners of dSLR cameras without full-frame sensors and who are considering buying a wide-angle lens, remember that it's important to take into account the crop factor of the sensor (see Crop Factor box, page 133). For example, the crop factor for most Nikon dSLRs is 1.5 – this means that in order to achieve an efl of 18mm, the lens needs to have a real focal length of 12mm (12 x 1.5 = 18mm).

COMPACT AND HYBRID WIDE ANGLE

You don't have to own a dSLR to get a really wide angle of view. As well as the main camera manufacturers, there are several third-party companies that make wide-angle converters, (such as the one pictured) to fit most compact or hybrid cameras, as long as the lens has a thread at the end. You'll need to know the size of the screw mount, and the angle of view the converter will provide will vary, but they typically range from x0.8 to x0.5. A x0.8 converter, for example, will change a 35mm focal length lens to 28mm.

Long Focal Length

Lenses with a focal length of between 80mm and 300mm are generally considered to have long focal lengths – although 400mm, 500mm and even 600mm focal length lenses are quite common. Such lenses are often referred to as telephoto lenses and cover an angle of view of between 28° (80mm) and 6° (400mm). It is a telephoto lens's narrow angle of view that creates the magnifying effect, for which there are numerous uses.

Sports and nature

Telephoto lenses are commonly used for sports and nature photography. The specific focal length needed depends on the type of nature or sports. It's often easier, for example, to get closer to the action when photographing tennis than it is with stadium sports such as football or track and field. Similarly,

photographing large mammals that are relatively accustomed to humans and to which the photographer can get close requires less telephoto power than photographing small birds.

◀ **LEFT** A long focal length can be used to great effect to record details that might otherwise get lost in a wider picture.

There are a number of zoom compacts offering 10x magnification, (which is roughly the equivalent of efl 30–300mm), and this should provide most keen amateurs with the magnification that they need. For dSLR owners, with zoom lenses that are now capable of resolving and capturing almost as much detail as prime lenses, the best option is to opt for a 70–300mm lens, which will provide a useful telephoto range, particularly if the camera's crop factor is taken into account. A 300mm focal length with a 1.6 crop factor provides an efl of 480mm. Even professional sports and nature photographers rarely use lenses longer than 500mm

▲ **ABOVE** Shooting sports often requires the use of a telephoto lens; however, many telephoto lens have a minimum aperture of f/5.6 or even f/8, for example, which means a relatively slow shutter speed will be needed to ensure an accurate exposure.

▲ **ABOVE** The long telephoto lens is essential equipment for all wildlife photographers, allowing them to get 'close' to the action without disturbing the animals or risking their own safety.

▲ **ABOVE** Using a telephoto lens for portraits allows you to easily throw potentially distracting backgrounds out of focus.

▲ **ABOVE** For candid street photography, a telephoto lens is the perfect choice as it allows you to keep your distance from your subject.

– their enormous size is down to the fact that they're extremely fast lenses that are often able to open up to apertures as wide as f/2.8.

Landscapes and candid shots

Surprisingly, a telephoto lens can also be a useful addition to the landscape photographer's kit. One of the key characteristics of long focal lengths is that scenes are foreshortened, so that distant, rolling hills take on a pleasing layered effect. In addition, landscape photographers can isolate and enlarge particularly attractive visual elements of a scene with a telephoto lens. Effectively, this is the case for all genres of photography. Telephotos are excellent at helping the photographer to fill the frame and the great benefit of using a zoom telephoto is that it's possible to frame shots in camera, rather than having to crop them at a later date on the computer.

Another use for a telephoto lens (in this case the more discreet the better), is in candid street photography. You'll have only a very short amount of time to frame and take the shot, but the results can be rewarding as the photographer will often capture an action or expression that becomes apparent only when reviewing the image on screen.

Portraits

Finally, short telephoto lenses of between efl 80mm and 130mm make excellent portrait lenses. In fact, in the early days of photography, such telephoto lenses were often referred to as 'portrait' lenses. They're good for the job because they not only help to distance the sitter from the photographer (so making the sitter feel less self-conscious), but the longer focal length also has the effect of flattening the subject's features very slightly. This results in a more flattering portrait and, when combined with a wide aperture, the narrow depth of field ensures that backgrounds are more easily thrown out of focus.

▼ **BELOW** This 70–300mm 'super zoom' covers a wide range of telephoto focal lengths in a single lens. Vibration-reduction technology helps avoid camera shake.

maximum aperture

focus distance

zoom ring

Focal Length and Backgrounds

In the earlier section on depth of field we discussed how, together with the lens's aperture setting and the focusing distance, the third factor governing depth of field was focal length. Now that we've examined focal length in more detail, let's return to the relationship between depth of field and focal length and look more closely at how adjusting focal length can be used to alter backgrounds.

Focal length and depth of field

As we know, a short focal length lens of efl 28mm set at f/5.6, for example, will have a zone of sharpness almost twice as wide as an efl 50mm lens set at the same aperture. This is why it's often advantageous to use a telephoto lens for portraits, as it's easier to throw a potentially distracting background out of focus with a longer focal length lens. You just have to walk farther back from your subject, zoom in so that you achieve the same shot and retake the picture – the longer the focal length the more blurred the background. However, it's not just depth of field that alters with focal length; you can also use varying focal lengths to alter the actual view of the background.

Altering viewpoint

A popular camera trick in the movies – one that's often used to promote a sense of unease or panic – is to show the subject standing still, but the background viewpoint changing from narrow to wide or vice versa. The technique is known as a dolly zoom, and was made famous by Alfred Hitchcock in his movie *Vertigo*. To achieve the shot, the camera tracks back or forward on rails while at the same time zooming in or out. This way, the size and view of the subject remains unchanged, but because the

▲ **ABOVE** By using a wide-angle lens with a narrow aperture, everyone from the girl in the foreground to the man in the background is sharply in focus, creating a feeling of unity.

focal length and, therefore, angle of view are changing as the camera zooms in and out, the background viewpoint and perspective also change. This trick can also be used by stills photographers to great effect.

▼ **BELOW** Using a long focal length lens or setting makes it easier to throw the foreground and background out of focus, so concentrating the viewer's attention on the subject.

The effect works on the basis that in a photograph, objects closer to the camera appear disproportionately larger than those positioned farther away. So with a short focal length lens and the subject positioned close to the camera, the subject will appear exaggerated in size and the background far in the distance – this can often be used to create a sense of isolation. Moving back, using a long focal length and filling the same amount of frame with the subject, the background will appear much closer to the subject and relatively larger in size – in this shot the subject would appear much more part of his or her surroundings. This is partly due to the foreshortening effect of long focal length lenses.

Selecting background

Knowing that focal length alters view-point helps you to exclude or include background elements in a shot while the subject remains the same size. Also, since the angle of view affected is vertical as well as horizontal, a steeper perspective is also provided by a close camera view, which can be used to help isolate detail (see pages 140–141).

ABOVE AND ABOVE RIGHT By adjusting his viewpoint and zooming in slightly, the photographer has successfully isolated the tower so that it stands out more from the background.

BELOW By getting low to the ground and using a short focal length setting or wide-angle lens pointing upward, these pigeons are clearly silhouetted against the sky, creating a dramatic shot.

Focal Length – Try It Yourself

These exercises are designed to explore how varying focal length will affect images. The first exercise shows how focal length affects depth of field, while the second will show how focal length can be used to effectively change background viewpoints.

It's helpful if you have the camera on a tripod, as that way it's easier to set up the shots and compare the results, and you don't have to worry about slow shutter speeds if you're shooting in dim lighting conditions.

Depth of field

On a small area of land, set up two objects about 10 ft (3m) apart. Place the camera around 13 ft (4m) in front of the first object. The distances don't really matter – all that's important is that, with focal lengths ranging from 35mm (efl) and 170mm (efl), you can see both objects clearly. Now, with the

> ▼ **BELOW** For these three pictures, the lens was zoomed out as the photographer moved closer to the subject to match the framing. Notice how the longer focal length compresses the foreground and background areas.

zoom set to around 170mm, frame the front object so that it fills around half the height of the viewfinder and focus on it (making sure the rear object is still clearly visible). With the camera set to Aperture priority, choose the widest aperture and take a shot. Without moving the camera, zoom out to around 80–100mm and take another shot. Finally, zoom out to around 28–35mm and fire the shutter once more.

To see the shots at their best, you ideally need to download them onto a computer and crop the second and third shots so that they show more or less the same scene as the first – that is, the front object filling half the height of the viewfinder. You'll be cropping right into the third shot, but don't worry about the image quality – all you're assessing is depth of field.

With all three images showing approximately the same scene, the rear object should be entirely out of focus in the 170mm focal length shot, in the 80–100mm picture the rear object should be more sharply defined, while the final shot – taken at 28–35mm – should show both objects in focus.

38mm

Changing viewpoint

For the second exercise you'll need a slightly larger area to work in, and the greater the difference between the shortest and longest focal length lens, the more apparent the results. The images shown were shot with a 35–170mm (efl) zoom and show the effect well. Use a tripod if you have one so the camera doesn't move between shots.

Begin by picking an object between 3 and 7ft (1m and 2m) tall – a family member or friend is ideal. Position

170mm

80mm

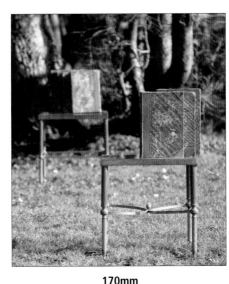

80mm

170mm

◀ **LEFT** Taken using 38mm, 80mm and 170mm focal lengths these three images were then cropped to the same size. Notice how by increasing the focal length it reduces the depth of field, making the books that are farther away out of focus.

▼ **BELOW RIGHT** Increasing the focal length can often be a more practical alternative to getting physically closer to the subject, particularly when taking shots of wild animals. Here a 500mm telephoto lens was used to get close to the doe and her calf.

your subject so there is variety and recognizable depth to the background, such as a tree at one distance, a hedge at another and a fence at a third. As long as you can see the relative distances between the objects it doesn't matter what they are.

Set the zoom to the longest focal length and position yourself so that the object fills the bottom half of the frame before taking a shot. Then, zoom out to half the original focal length, but also walk closer to the subject

(trying to stay in line with the background), so that it still fills roughly the bottom half of the viewfinder and take another shot. Finally, repeat the exercise, but zoom out to the shortest focal length (widest angle) that your lens offers. Walk toward the subject, fill half the frame once again, and take a final shot.

Download the images onto a computer and review them carefully. It ought to be apparent how, in the longest focal length shot, the

background appears to be compressed and the angle of view narrow. With the second and third shots, although the size of the subject should have remained more or less the same, you will see that the background appears to stretch out away from the subject, and the space between the various background objects should be increasingly well delineated. Notice also, however, how the angle of view is both wider and taller as you zoom out with your lens.

38mm

Close Up and Macro

With the great improvement in lens technology – which is apparent on both fixed-lens compact and hybrid cameras, as well as lenses for dSLRs – an increasing number of people have become fascinated with taking photographs of small, sometimes tiny, objects using the macro feature on the camera or lens.

True macro

Before looking at some of the equipment and techniques that will help you capture great close ups, it's important to differentiate between macro and close-up photography. Strictly speaking, macro photography involves being able to project an image onto the sensor the same size as the subject itself, in other words at a scale of 1:1. Over time, however, this definition has been relaxed somewhat, so that today lenses capable of projecting an image half the size of the original object (1:2) are widely considered macro. Many camera and lens manufacturers have gone even further, and have started to label lenses with only 1:4 magnification as 'macro', although these lenses aren't

strictly macro, they simply have the ability to focus 'close up', enabling the photographer to capture the object in close detail.

At the other end of the scale, there are some macro lenses that are almost scientific instruments, having the ability to capture images at 5:1, or five times larger than the size of the original object.

Equipment

If you're a dSLR owner, for the best results and in terms of ease of use, a dedicated macro lens is the best option. Such a lens will retain all the usual functions, such as autofocus, auto metering and complete depth of

field control, as well as providing excellent results. Macro lenses are available in focal lengths ranging from around 50mm to 180mm. The longer the focal length, the farther you can be from the subject while still being able to capture true 1:1 macro shots. This has its benefits when shooting insects, for example, which may fly away at the sight of an approaching camera lens. Remember to take into account the camera's crop factor before deciding on a specific lens – a 60mm focal length on most

LEFT A 'true' macro photograph allows you to image the subject at a ratio of 1:1 on your sensor, but some lenses allow even greater enlargement.

▼ **BELOW** The narrow depth of field common to many macro shots is often apparent in advertising images.

Macro tools

For the highest quality results, a dedicated macro lens for your dSLR is the best, but most expensive, option. Alternatives include extension, rings that fit between your normal lens and the camera to enable close focusing, or a reversing ring that allows you to attach the lens 'back to front'. Although cheaper, both options can mean you have to focus manually and may also mean you have to set the aperture manually as well.

Macro Lens

Extension Tube

dSLRs will have an efl of around 90mm, for example. While designed specifically for macro shots, the majority of macro lenses also make excellent portrait lenses. The efl of 90–100mm (the most common macro focal length) is long enough to create flattering portraits and usually such lenses are quite 'fast', with a maximum aperture of around f/2.8.

Reversing rings
A much less expensive option to a dedicated macro lens is a reversing ring. As its name suggests, this device allows you to attach the front of the lens to the camera body, which has the effect of greatly magnifying the subject. Although good results can be achieved with reversing rings, you may find that you'll have to focus manually and that the aperture closes down as you adjust it, resulting in a dark viewfinder. This makes it much harder both to frame and focus potential shots.

Extension tubes
More expensive than a reversing ring, but again much less expensive than a dedicated macro lens, are extension tubes. These non-optical devices increase the distance between the sensor and the lens, thus allowing the lens to focus closer to the subject.

Extension tubes work with a variety of focal length lenses and can provide good results.

Hybrids and compacts
Some excellent close-up photography can be taken with hybrid and compact cameras. This is because the small image sensor only requires lenses with a very short focal length, which in turn means you can get very close to the subject and keep it in focus.

Manual focus
No matter what type of camera you're using, it may be much easier to turn off the camera's autofocus setting and focus manually on the subject. Rather than using the focus ring or focus buttons, set the focus close to the point you want to be sharpest, and move your entire upper torso nearer to or farther away from the subject, until you achieve the focus you want.

Tripod support
A common problem with macro photography is the extremely narrow depth of field you get. This can be used to the photographer's advantage by adding impact to an image, but

▷ RIGHT Even with modern autofocus systems, macro focusing can still be quite tricky, so try using manual focus.

▲ ABOVE LEFT In macro photography, the depth of field becomes very shallow, allowing you to pick out the tiniest part of your subject.

▲ ABOVE Manually setting the focus point close to the area you want sharp and then moving forward and back until you achieve focus works well.

it does mean carefully considering the subject before deciding which elements should be sharp.

One way of increasing depth of field is to use a small aperture and long exposure. For this you will require a tripod, and the object being photographed has to remain perfectly still during the entire exposure.

Filters

In recent times, with ever more sophisticated image-editing software on the market, an ever-increasing number of photographers are turning to the digital darkroom to replicate the effects of lens filters. So does this spell the end for lens filters?

Lens filters are made of glass or plastic. They either screw onto the end of the lens, or are part of a kit that features a filter holder and an adapter ring that screws onto the end of the lens, to which the filter holder then clips. The former tend to be circular, while the latter can be square and simply slide into a slot in the filter holder.

All dSLR lenses and many hybrid camera lenses can accept lens filters – look for a screw thread on the end of the lens. Screw-in filters come in various diameters, ranging from around 45mm up to 95mm, and filter holder kits usually come in similar sizes. There should be a label on the front of the lens indicating that lens's specific filter size. Some compact cameras may also feature a lens with a screw thread.

Colour filters

Traditionally, when used with film cameras, colour filters were used either to correct a colour cast caused by artificial light or to add an overall colour to an image – neither of which could be easily carried out in the darkroom after the image had been shot.

The use of colour filters to correct colour casts when shooting digitally is certainly still possible, but if you're shooting in RAW, you're likely to achieve a more accurate colour-corrected image by editing it on computer. Similarly, using a colour filter to 'warm up' (make slightly more red) or 'cool' down (make slightly more blue) an image is possible, and

many photographers – even when shooting digitally – will still use this method. However, equally good results are again possible on the computer, and this also provides a much greater level of control in terms of both the specific colour and its strength.

Yet while much can be done in post-production to replicate the effect of certain filters, there are a number of filters that you may still want to consider purchasing.

Ultraviolet (UV) filters

Fitting a UV filter to a lens is worth considering, not so much for its inherent optical properties, but for the protection it affords the lens. The aim of a UV filter is to reduce the amount of ultraviolet light entering the lens, which can cause haziness in certain situations. Because such filters are usually clear they can be left on the lens and won't have any impact on the colour or tone of the image. Many photographers fit such filters to protect the front element of the lens, as it's much cheaper to

ABOVE These two shots show the effect of a polarizing filter. Without such a filter (top) reflections, which render the glass milky white, are clearly apparent in the glass table top. With a polarizing filter attached to the lens (bottom) the reflections disappear and the glass becomes more transparent.

LEFT Polarizing filters should be considered as almost essential for landscape photography. Not only will they cut reflections, but they can also make skies appear bluer.

LEFT Like a polarizing filter, a graduated neutral density filter is ideal for landscape photography, allowing you to balance bright skies with darker foreground areas.

replace a filter than to have a scratch removed from an expensive lens. In addition, frequently wiping a filter is preferable to constantly cleaning the lens, which may damage the lens coating over time.

Polarizing filters

A polarizing filter is one example where the effect of the filter cannot be replicated easily on a computer. Such filters behave in exactly the same way as the polarizing lenses in a pair of sunglasses, in that they cut down on reflected light and reduce glare and haze. While these optical properties are often exploited in photography, polarizing filters can also be used to add contrast to blue, cloudy skies (making the sky bluer and the clouds whiter) and can boost the general colour saturation in an image as well.

Due to the overall darkening effect of polarizing filters, it's important to be aware that exposure can be reduced by one or two stops. In other words, a landscape that needs an exposure of f/16 at $^1/_{125}$ sec, may need an exposure of f/16 at $^1/_{60}$ sec or $^1/_{30}$ sec, or f/11 or f/8 at $^1/_{125}$ sec when it's taken using a polarizer filter – or you could increase the ISO setting one or two steps.

If you're seriously considering adding a polarizer filter to your kit, ensure that you buy a circular polarizer. There are linear polarizers on the market, but the way in which they filter the light can sometimes stop a camera's metering and autofocusing systems from functioning properly.

Graduated neutral density filters

Another group of filters that all professional landscape photographers carry with them are graduated neutral density filters. These are a neutral grey at the top, graduating to clear at the bottom. Their purpose is to overcome the common issue of exposing for both bright sky and darker land. With such a large dynamic range, often either the sky is overexposed and the land correctly exposed, or the sky correctly exposed and the land underexposed. By using a graduated neutral density filter, you can expose for the land, while the grey element (the 'neutral density') at the top half of the filter prevents the sky from being overexposed.

Graduated neutral density filters come in a variety of 'strengths', with darker or lighter grey being used depending on the brightness levels of the sky. As well as graduated grey filters, they are also available in a range of colours such as red, blue and yellow.

Plain neutral density filters

You can also get plain neutral density (ND) filters, which are uniformly grey. By reducing the amount of light reaching the sensor (without affecting colour), such filters allow for a longer exposure or narrower depth of field, both of which can be used creatively in certain circumstances. Like the graduated filters, ND filters are available in a variety of 'strengths' – ND2, ND4 and ND8 – that reduce exposure by one, two and three stops.

RIGHT Neutral density filters reduce the amount of light coming through the lens and reaching the sensor, giving slower shutter speeds that can be used creatively.

Photojournalism – It's Not Just Art

Up until now, we've concentrated on learning as much as we can about the intricacies of how a digital camera works; how to get the best possible results from it using manual and semi-manual modes and how to improve photographs through the application of some basic tips and hints on composition. This will help you to take photographs that are optimally exposed and have aesthetic merit in terms of their composition.

However, as well as the beautifully composed shot, always look out for images that will hold the viewer's attention in other ways. This may be through humour or poignancy, or through a specific issue the image raises. Frequently, you may only have a fraction of a second to capture the image – in which case the best policy may be to select Auto and fire away. You may not end up with the most creative exposure, but if you don't have time to consider the scene carefully, Auto should at least provide a reasonably accurate exposure and well-focused shot. And, once you've got a usable image, you can always switch to manual or semi-manual and try to improve on depth of field or exposure, if time allows.

Consider compact

Many professional photographers eschew their pro dSLR kit when they are out and about, in favour of a small compact camera. For grabbing quick, candid street shots while on the move, such a camera can certainly come into its own. Recent camera models start up and respond relatively quickly, and their size certainly makes them far less conspicuous than a dSLR with a long zoom lens, and this allows you to wander around more or less unnoticed. You might not have

 ABOVE As well as technically competent photographs, always keep an eye out for unusual subjects, such as this 'giant' staring out from behind the doors.

BELOW These children are completely unaware of the camera in this image. Candid shots are much easier to obtain if you are using a compact than if you are wielding a bulky, professional-looking dSLR.

quite the same creative control as you do with a dSLR, but at least you'll be able to record what's going on around you well enough.

It's worth getting into the habit of taking a camera with you wherever you go, even if you don't have a specific photographic opportunity in mind. It's likely that you'll find something worth photographing during the course of each day, and getting into the habit of looking for and assessing potential scenes will help you with just about every aspect of your photography.

Photographers' rights

What you can and cannot legally photograph varies enormously from country to country. If you're in any doubt, seek advice or permission from people who you trust – this may well be embassy or consulate staff if you're travelling abroad. If you plan to shoot a specific famous landmark, it pays to contact the owner or the people responsible for the property to ask for their permission first. If you're concerned about simply walking around a city or large town taking photographs, you may find some helpful advice at a tourist information centre.

Historically in the UK, USA and in most of Europe, photography would attract little attention. Photographers could happily walk around large cities taking pictures of major landmarks without fear of attracting the notice of either security staff or the police. Now, however, due to increased security awareness, photographers often find themselves being confronted by the authorities. While legally you're perfectly within your rights to photograph buildings and people in public places, you'll find that in larger cities you may be asked who you are and what you're doing. You may even find that attempts will be made to seize your equipment. Only a police officer is legally

entitled to seize property and then he or she has to be making an arrest; the police cannot seize property without a court order. If you're asked to hand over equipment to security staff, politely but firmly ask for their names and under what authority they're acting. If they refuse to tell you, but persist in demanding the equipment and won't let you simply leave, call the police.

▶ **RIGHT** Political rallies and marches can often provide strong graphic images. In these situations you may find a compact camera attracts less attention than a dSLR.

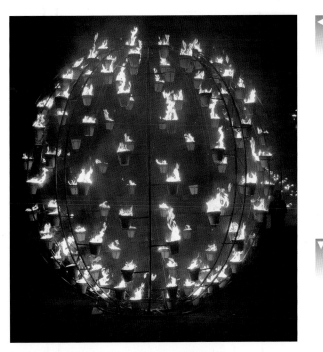

◀ **LEFT** Many modern compacts are capable of capturing an acceptable image even in the most difficult lighting circumstances, so it pays to have one with you all the time in case you come across unexpected events such as this fire display.

▼ **BELOW** If you carry a camera with you at all times you'll be in the position to take a picture of anything that interests you, such as this shop window display.

Black and White

Although technological advances have been the catalyst for a transition from black and white to colour in both television and the movies, and similar technological advances have made it possible for us now to capture and print accurate colour photographs, black and white photography is still very much alive and kicking. There are numerous websites, magazines and books devoted to the art of black and white photography and, for many, the black and white image is the pinnacle of art photography.

Colour photography can, in many ways, be seen simply as a way of capturing and conveying an image of the world around us – as beautiful or as shocking as it may be – because most of us see the world in colour. A black and white image, however, is already one step removed from 'reality', and so it immediately becomes less a way of simply conveying a scene, and more about conveying the photographer's interpretation of the scene. The same applies for colour photography, of course, but even more so with black and white photography, which is why it is and will always remain such a popular genre.

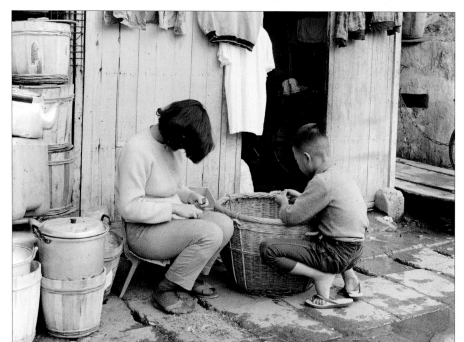

TOP Removing colour often helps us to reveal nature's extraordinary forms and shapes more clearly.

ABOVE Black and white images can often convey a greater sense of gravitas or austerity than colour.

LEFT For many photographers, black and white is the only medium for street photography, immediately giving pictures a 'gritty' newspaper look.

Digital black and white

Traditionally, with film cameras, the photographer had to decide whether to shoot on black and white or colour film, and once the decision had been made, it was impossible to change. With digital imaging you are no longer forced to make that decision. If you want, you can shoot everything in colour and decide at a later stage which images are potential candidates for black and white conversion.

While there's nothing inherently wrong with this approach, it can make for a slightly hit or miss approach to black and white, and it's far better to know in advance what ingredients you need for a good black and white composition. There's no doubting that for most photographers used to working in colour, switching to black and white can come as something of a surprise. Until we start shooting black and white, we are unaware of how reliant we are on colour to make our images work, and that's a very good reason to spend at least some time 'thinking', and if at all possible shooting, specifically in black and white.

Shooting black and white

Most cameras have a black and white mode, and although this isn't the best way of capturing black and white images, using this setting when you're next out with your camera is an excellent exercise as it provides you

with an instant black and white preview. To obtain the best black and white results, shoot in RAW if you have the option, as this will retain much more tonal information than shooting JPEG.

However, if you print directly from your camera, you'll have to shoot black and white JPEGs. Although these will provide adequate black and white prints, you won't have the same level of control compared with converting the images on a computer.

Over the next few pages, we'll be looking at ways of learning how to best compose for black and white photography. Not only is this essential if you're to produce attention-grabbing black and white images, but it will also prove enormously helpful whenever you revert to colour photography.

Noise

When shooting in black and white, or for black and white conversion, it's even more important to set the lowest possible ISO than it is when shooting in colour. The reason for this is that noise is more evident in dark tones, such as dark greys and blacks, than in any other colour, particularly in low-light photography.

TOP This gorgeous shot is all about the soft tones in the image, which have been enhanced by a gentle blur and a slow shutter speed smoothing the water.

ABOVE Black and white portraits can often be far more powerful than their colour counterparts.

LEFT Shooting in black and white forces you to concentrate on tone and texture, avoiding the potential distraction of colour.

Black and White Composition

Without colour, it's inevitable that other elements of composition must come to the fore for a black and white image to be successful. This is the beauty and challenge of black and white photography, and the reason why so many people hold it in such high esteem. It forces us to be more aware and to look much more closely at potential subjects.

Tone, shape and texture

Without colour, it's crucial that the subtleties of tone are captured in as much detail as possible, and for this it's doubly important to be aware of the quality of light at different times of the day or year. Morning and late afternoon will usually provide light that best draws out the subtlety of the tones, but that's not to say that strong, midday light is inappropriate for black and white photography. With the sun high in the sky, shape is emphasized and – depending on the angle of light in relation to the

subject – texture can also be clearer. Furthermore, with harsh light, you'll find that you can achieve a greater dynamic range; whites tend to be whiter and blacks darker. Given the right subject matter, the presence of strong blacks and strong whites – with little greyscale in between – can result in a powerful graphic image.

Over time, you'll appreciate how light impacts on black and white imagery in different ways to colour. For example, you'll quickly discover that dull light that may be unsuitable for colour photography because colours are rendered uninteresting and drab, is ideal for black and white as it allows the photographer to explore and emphasize the tones of a scene without fear of harsh,

complicating shadows and blown highlights. Similarly, such light is often best for shooting portraits, as the tones are more flattering and the reduced contrast allows the intricate form of a face to be fully represented.

Pattern

One aspect of composition that does not rely too heavily on the prevailing lighting conditions is pattern. You can seek out appropriate patterns for potential black and white treatment whether the light is harsh or soft. For many photographers, the repetitious nature of pattern is made stronger without the distracting presence of colour, which in many scenes could be the only way that one element is differentiated from another.

RIGHT The lack of colour in this shot of St Basil's Cathedral, Moscow, encourages the viewer to concentrate not only on the form and texture of the domes, but also on the spaces in between the domes.

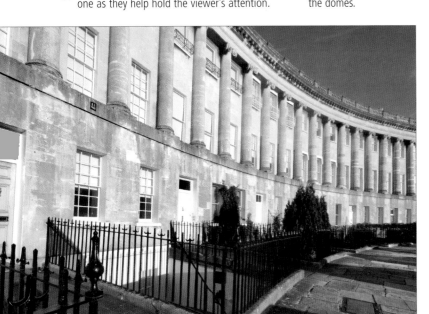
BELOW Strong lines are even more important in a black and white picture than a colour one as they help hold the viewer's attention.

▲ **ABOVE** Without colour, the form, shape and tones of a subject take on a much greater significance if you want the viewer to be able to 'read', or interpret, an image successfully.

▲ **ABOVE** With strong shadows, it's possible to create striking images in black and white pictures that might not have as much impact in colour.

Horizontals, verticals and curves

Without colour, another way of keeping the viewer's attention is to look for strong leading lines to guide the viewer around the image. Although leading lines are important in colour photography, they can be the key to a good black and white image and the stronger they are, the less the image is about representing a recognizable scene, and the more it becomes a visual statement.

Tonal contrast

Perhaps the hardest aspect of 'seeing' in black and white is forcing yourself to differentiate between tonal contrast and colour contrast. For example, reds and blues are on the opposite sides of the colour wheel and therefore contrast strongly, but when they are converted to black and white that contrast may well be diminished, or even lost altogether. When working in black and white, it's important to remember that it's not the hue of a colour that's important, but its brightness value.

While the rules of composition for colour and black and white photography are pretty much identical, you'll find at first that you have to work that little bit harder to get black and white images

that you're happy with. But, after a while, seeing potential black and white scenes should become second nature, while shooting them in colour and converting them on computer will give you the option of having two versions of the same scene. It will also give more control over the black and white conversion process.

▼ **BELOW** Although the subject of a silhouette is always black, silhouettes can often work better as black and white images as they have no distracting background colour.

Composition

Colour in composition can be a help as well as a hindrance. Without colour to fall back on, you will need to work much harder to take black and white photographs that have real impact. Always be on the look-out for strong leading lines, patterns, textures and shapes in a potential image, as well as subtleties of light and shade and tone.

Black and White – Try It Yourself

There are no short cuts to taking successful black and white images; it's a skill that develops over time and with experience. As we've seen, although more or less the same 'rules' of composition apply to black and white photography as well as colour, you really do have to plan a black and white composition more, and ask yourself exactly what it is that you're trying to achieve with the shot.

Comparative shots

The best way to start experimenting with black and white photography is to return to local places where in the past you have taken some successful colour shots. Replicate as closely as possible the shots that worked well and re-photograph them using the camera's black and white mode.

Download the images on to your computer and compare them on screen with prints that you have of the colour images. Alternatively, if you have image-editing software, try converting some of your favourite images into black and white.

Don't worry if the black and white images look nowhere near as good as the colour versions, the purpose of the exercise isn't to go out and take stunning black and white images, the purpose really is to compare the two sets to see how the compositional elements translate into black and white. Look to see how the colours have converted into different shades of grey. Examine the images to see if shape and form are emphasized in the black and white versions. Does the absence of colour change the overall atmosphere of the images?

▶ **RIGHT** The age and scale of this building in Prague lend themselves to a black and white image, taking us back to a bygone era.

Shoot black and white

Having carried out the comparative test, you should be a little more aware of what makes a good black and white composition. The next time you're out with your camera, make a deliberate point of shooting for black and white only. Aspects that should be at the forefront of your mind are:

• Texture and tone – look out for objects or scenes that have a good gradation of tone, from very dark greys to light whites. Try to shoot under varied lighting to see how it can affect the overall contrast of an image. Return to the same scene but under different lighting conditions to compare the effect of harsh, high-contrasting with soft, low-contrasting light. Look for objects and scenes that feature texture so apparent that you can almost 'feel' it just by sight.

• Pattern and shape – a lack of colour can emphasize rather than detract from pattern. There are numerous artificial as well as natural objects and scenes that reveal pattern often in quite unexpected ways. Also look out for objects with well-defined and interesting shapes – in a similar way to pattern, these can also benefit from being captured in black and white.

• If you're an avid landscape photographer, look out for blue skies with plenty of white clouds. Famous American photographer Ansel Adams is perhaps most famous for his black and white landscapes, many of which featured dark, almost black, skies with broad sweeps of white cloud. Use a polarizing filter to enhance the contrast between the sky and clouds.

• Leading lines and curves are important in colour photography, but they are often even more essential in black and white photography; look out for scenes with strong diagonals, verticals, horizontals and curves. These visual guides can lead the viewer through an image and provide the image with graphic elements.

▲▲ **ABOVE AND ABOVE RIGHT** Converting some of your images on computer is a good way to begin to learn what works well as a black and white shot. Here, the juxtaposition of the structures of the trees and the fence – one natural, one artificial – is more apparent in the monochrome shot; so, too, are the sweeping shadows.

▶ **RIGHT AND FAR RIGHT** The purpose of these images is to compare the sense of texture between the colour image and the black and white, between both the stones and the clouds above.

◀ **LEFT AND BELOW** In the black and white version the dappled light is still apparent and the image assumes a more abstract quality.

Shooting for Manipulation

Most amateur digital photographers (and all professionals) use computers and image-editing software as part of their photographic workflow today. Often this will be for the purpose of standard editing, such as sharpening, cropping or adjusting white balance or contrast, particularly if the images have been shot RAW, in which case no in-camera processing will have occurred and the images will need to undergo such basic editing processes before they can be printed.

There are a number of occasions when photographers will shoot images in the knowledge that they will be manipulated on a computer at a later date – during the process often referred to as post-production.

High-dynamic range

One of the most common occasions when photographers will deliberately shoot for post-production is when the dynamic range in the scene exceeds the camera sensor's ability to capture it. If, for example, due to a bright sky and dark land, the sensor is unable to record both highlights and shadow regions without either the former 'blowing out' or the latter 'filling in' and losing all shadow detail, then often the best course of action is to take two shots – one exposed for the sky and one exposed for the land – and compose them on computer as one image that successfully renders the entire tonal range of the scene.

RAW

Shooting in RAW allows you to adjust the exposure on a computer later and thus create two images (one each for the sky and land) that can be merged as one file. In many ways it increases the dynamic range of the sensor, but the difference between the highlights and shadows is often so great that the extra exposure compensation added in post-production is such that you run the risk of introducing noise into the darkest areas of the image – those most prone to noise.

Panoramas

Photographers will often deliberately shoot for post-production when they want to create panoramas. In such instances, the photographer will take two, three or even more slightly overlapping shots of a panoramic scene, often with the aid of a tripod to ensure the images are aligned accurately. Later the images can then be downloaded and 'stitched' together to form one long panorama.

LEFT AND BELOW A very good reason to keep a small library of different types of sky – stormy, cloudy or sunny – is that you never know when you'll want to superimpose a more interesting sky over a good shot with a dull sky; but be aware of the ethical compromise.

▶ RIGHT Digital photography combined with a computer and some basic image-editing software makes photomontage quick and easy. A quick trawl through your catalogue of images will throw up endless possibilities.

Most examples of image-editing software feature commands that partially automate the process of merging the images together by looking for repeated 'patterns' of a scene from each shot and laying them on top of the other.

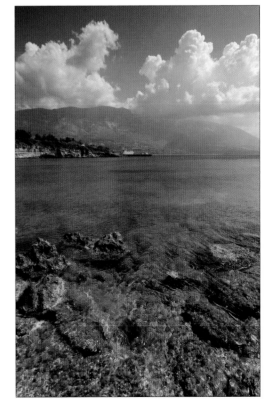

Photomontage

The third common reason for shooting for post-production is to create photomontages. This fairly old technique has been around more or less since the advent of photography and involves merging two or more, often incongruent, images together to make one image. In conventional film photography, this was usually only achieved by carefully cutting out the various components with a craft knife and assembling them on the main background image – with mixed results. With today's powerful image-editing software, featuring sophisticated cut-out tools, Layers and Blending Modes, it's now much easier to merge images together seamlessly to create all too credible scenes.

Image libraries

Now that photographers are able to potentially merge two images together seamlessly, many have 'libraries' of image elements, such as sunsets, blue cloudy skies, deserted beaches and so

on, which they add when they have the option of photographing a potentially useful element. In this way, they can replace, for example, a slightly dull-looking sky in a particular shot with a much more photogenic one, to give the whole image a makeover.

Ethics

Inevitably, there are certain ethical issues affecting image manipulation. One professional photographer was struck off a well-known news service for slightly increasing the density of palls of smoke following an explosion to give the image an added sense of drama. A similar effect could have been achieved using traditional techniques in a darkroom, but the fear of digital image manipulation in

professional circles is so great that draconian punishments are often meted out. Naturally, for amateur photographers who are displaying their photographs for family and friends, there's not an issue, but it may become one if images are entered into competitions and the rules strictly state that only minor enhancements to images are allowed.

▶ RIGHT Combining one shot exposed for the foreground with a second exposed for the sky can be an effective way of obtaining an image with a high dynamic range – useful if you don't have a grey graduated filter to hand. But you will need a tripod or something sturdy on which to rest the camera.

Glossary

A

AEL (auto exposure lock) A means, usually in the form of a button, of retaining the exposure setting read from one part of a scene. The shot can then be reframed if necessary while ensuring the previously metered element of the scene will be accurately exposed.

Aperture The size of the opening in a lens that governs how much light reaches the sensor (or film).

Aperture priority (A/Av) A semi-automatic exposure setting in which the photographer selects the aperture and the camera determines and sets an appropriate shutter speed to achieve an accurate exposure.

Autofocus (AF) A setting in which the camera's lens is able to focus automatically on a specific part of a scene. All modern cameras have an autofocus function.

B

Bit (binary digit) The basic unit of all digital data; bits are either 'on' or 'off' and represented by the numbers '1' and '0'.

Bracketing A technique in which a variety of exposures, usually three, is made in very quick succession of a particular scene in order to ensure correct exposure.

C

CCD (charge coupled device) One of the two most common types of sensor used today in digital cameras and scanners.

CMOS (complementary metal oxide semiconductor) The second-most commonly used sensor (after CCD) in digital cameras and scanners.

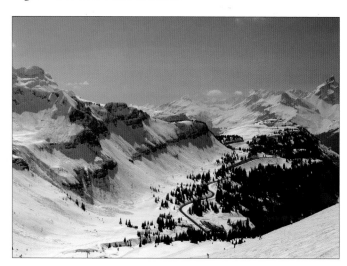

Colour filter array (CFA) A very thin coloured matrix layer that sits above the sensor layer in a digital camera's imaging sensor to enable the sensor to record colour. CFAs feature a matrix of red, green and blue squares.

Compression A method of reducing digital file sizes, such as image files, while retaining as much significant information as possible in order to ensure as high as possible image quality. There are two types of compression: 'lossy' compression, such as that used in JPEG files, discards information that cannot be retrieved – in effect, the higher the compression the lower the image quality. Lossy compression can result in very small files sizes. In 'lossless' compression, such as that used in TIFF files, information is bundled or 'zipped' temporarily while the file is stored, and then unzipped when opened. No information is lost with this compression technique, resulting in high-quality but large image files.

D

Depth of field A term used to described an image's 'zone of sharpness', or how much of the image is in focus. The main way to control depth of field is via the lens aperture.

Digital zoom A function offered by many compact cameras. It works by digitally increasing the size of the pixels being recorded by the sensor, as opposed to an optical zoom, which magnifies the image through a series of lenses before it reaches the sensor. Increasing the size of the pixels can result in poor image quality, and for this reason digital zoom should be used only when there's no alternative.

Dpi (dots per inch) Measurement of the resolution of an output device, such as a printer. See also Ppi (pixels per inch).

Dynamic range The optical range in a scene between the brightest (highlight) and darkest (shadow) areas in which detail is still visible.

E

Equivalent focal length (efl) is the optical focal length of the lens once the size of the sensor is taken into account. The smaller the sensor the longer the effective focal length of the lens.

Exposure The amount of light that reaches a camera's sensor or film. It is governed by the size of the aperture and for how long the shutter remains open (shutter speed).

Exposure compensation (EV) A way of manually overriding the built-in exposure meter of a camera to provide more or less light to the sensor or film.

F

Filter A glass or plastic attachment that fits on the front of the camera's lens. Filters are used for a variety of purposes: polarizing filters are used to reduce glare and reflections, while neutral density filters are used to reduce the light entering the lens.

F number The measure of the aperture of a lens used for a specific shot. A low f number, such as f/2, indicates a large aperture, while a high number, such as f/32, indicates a very small aperture.

Focal length Strictly, the distance in millimetres between a lens's optical centre and the focal point. The focal length is an indication of the magnifying power of a lens.

H

Histogram A visual interpretation in the form of a graph that describes the tonal range of a given image.

I

Interpolation A digital means of artificially increasing the resolution of an image. There are various interpolation algorithms, but generally they all work on assessing adjacent pixels and introducing new pixels with similar tonal and colour values.

ISO (International Standards Organization) Historically, the measurement of the sensitivity of a specific film – the higher the ISO rating, the more sensitive the film. The rating has been adopted by digital camera manufacturers to reflect how sensitive the sensor is to light for any given shot.

J

JPEG (Joint Photographic Experts Group) One of the most commonly used file formats used by digital cameras for storing images.

K

Kelvin The unit of measurement used to describe light temperature.

L

LCD screen In digital cameras, the small screen usually found at the back of the camera, used to review (and preview) shots, and to provide information on the camera's settings.

Lens The light-capturing and focusing element of all digital cameras. Lenses usually contain a variety of individual elements that work together to direct and focus the light from the scene onto the sensor.

M

Macro A term used to loosely describe 'close-up' photography or lenses that have the ability to greatly magnify the subject.

Manual A term used to describe any part of the picture-taking process that involves the photographer's direct input. Manual exposure requires the photographer to set the aperture and the shutter speed based on the camera's, or an external light meter's, reading. Manual focus requires the photographer to decide manually on the point of focus. Taking manual control of the camera greatly increases the creative possibilities available.

Metering The system by which all cameras assesses exposure. There are various metering systems from simple spot metering to the more sophisticated evaluative, or matrix, metering.

Megapixel (MP) Literally, 1 million pixels. Megapixels are a measure of resolution most commonly used to describe the resolution of a camera's sensor or a specific image file.

N

Noise Interference of an electronic signal. In digital photography, noise manifests itself as unwanted artefacts in the form of clumps of discoloured pixels or a grain-like pattern in the captured image file.

O

Optical zoom See **Digital zoom.**

P

Pixel (picture element) The basic unit of all digital images; essentially a tiny square with its own hue, saturation and brightness values. Printed or viewed at an appropriate resolution, an image's individual pixels should be invisible to the naked eye. If an image is viewed or printed too large, it may assume a blocky appearance, known as pixelation.

Ppi (pixels per inch) The resolution of a digital image. The greater the ppi value, the higher the resolution.

Program An exposure option in which the camera automatically sets the shutter and aperture setting depending on the light meter reading. It differs from full Auto in that in program shift mode, the photographer can select any aperture/shutter exposure combinations based on the meter reading.

R

RAW A popular file format available in most digital cameras. RAW files are made up of unprocessed data as captured by the camera's sensor. For this reason, RAW files will usually need to undergo some form of image editing to obtain the optimum image.

Resolution The amount of detail visible in an image determined by the number of pixels. The term can also be applied to describe the resolving power of a lens.

RGB (red, green, blue) Primary colours which, when combined, are used to represent all the colours of the visible spectrum.

Rule of thirds A compositional technique used to promote the placement of the subject elements in key areas of the frame.

S

Shutter delay/lag The time between pressing the shutter release button and the camera taking the photograph. If sufficiently long, shutter delay can result in fast-moving objects moving out of the frame by the time the photograph is taken.

Shutter priority (S/Tv) A semi-automatic exposure setting in which the photographer selects the shutter speed and the camera automatically determines and sets an appropriate aperture setting to achieve an accurate exposure.

Shutter speed The time taken for the camera's shutter to open and close, thereby determining the period the sensor is exposed to the light. Some compacts don't have a shutter; the 'shutter speed' is represented by the sensor being turned on and off.

Stop The term used to describe an exposure value. Increasing an exposure by 1 stop, for example, involves doubling the amount of light reaching the sensor, which can be achieved by either increasing the aperture from f/5.6 to f/8, for example, or reducing the shutter speed from 1/500 sec to 1/250 sec.

T

TIFF (Tagged Image File Format) A popular file format available in most image-editing programs, but now used less on digital cameras. TIFF files use 'lossless' compression and therefore retain more image data.

U

USB (Universal Serial Bus) USB sockets and cables are the most common way of connecting printers, scanners and other devices to a computer.

W

White balance A system used in both cameras and image-editing software that helps to eradicate unwanted colour casts; in other words, white will appear white.

Z

Zone of sharpness See **Depth of field.**

Index

Acknowledgements

The publisher would like to thank the following for kindly supplying photographs for this book: Adam Juniper 126(bl, bc); Canon UK Ltd 12 (t), 19 (bl, br), 22 (tl, tr), 23 (t), 24 (tl, tr), 25 (tr, bl), 30 (bl), 31 (b), 126 (tl, tr), 142 (bc); Colin Barrett 31 (tr); Comstock 6 (c), 72 (tr); Corbis 3 (r), 5 (bl, br), 49 (bl), 51 (t), 64 (t), 94 (br), 104 (bl), 105 (tr), 111 (br), 121 (t), 130, 139 (b), 141 (br); Digital Vision 60 (bl); Fujifilm UK Ltd 20; ImageDJ 6 (br), 37 (b), 50 (br), 73 (tr) 117 (bl); Image Ideas 96 (br); Image 100 52 (br), 65 (br), 86 (t), 87 (t), 138 (t); iStock photography 49 ((br), 55 (cr, br), 60 (br), 61 (br), 68 (bl), 71 (tl), 73 (cr), 87 (tr), 126 (br), 136 (bl), 137 (tr), 147 (tr), 149 (cr, bl); Jupiter images 148 (bl); LaCie Ltd 159; Nikon UK Ltd 21, 22 (b), 25 (tl, br), 135 (b), 137 (b), 142 (bc); Panasonic UK Ltd 30 (t); Pentax UK Ltd 19 (tl, tr); Photodisk 4 (tl), 5 (bcl, bcr), 7(c, bl), 55 (t), 62 (b), 63 (tr), 64 (br), 65 (bl), 66 (t), 84 (b), 85 (cl, cr, b), 88, 90 (br),

113 (br), 119 (b), 122 (b), 124 (b), 128 (t, bl, br), 129 (t, c, b), 136 (br), 138 (b), 150 (br), 151 (b); Rubberball 90 (bl), 94 (bl), 96 (t); Sony Ericsson 18 (b).

All artwork by Jerry Fowler 12, 13, 21, 23, 24, 32, 33, 34, 39, 39, 77, 83, 132.

All other images by Steve Luck

Images are listed in clockwise order from the top (t = top, c = centre, b = bottom, r = right, l = left, tr = top right etc.).

Every effort has been made to obtain permission to reproduce copyright material, but there may be cases where we have been unable to trace a copyright holder. The publisher will be happy to correct any omissions in future printings.